# COGAT®
# GRADE 1
# MATH

3 Practice Tests
Level 7

Savant Test Prep™

www.SavantPrep.com

## Please leave a review for this book!

Thank you for purchasing this resource.

Please take a moment to leave a
review on the website where you purchased this.

# TABLE OF CONTENTS

# INTRODUCTION

## COGAT® GENERAL INFORMATION

- COGAT® stands for Cognitive Abilities Test®.
- The test measures students' reasoning skills and problem-solving skills.
- It provides educators with an overall assessment of students' academic strengths and weaknesses.
- The COGAT® is commonly used as a screener for gifted and talented programs.
  - Gifted and Talented (G&T) selection sometimes requires a teacher recommendation as well.
- The test is usually administered in a group setting.
- A teacher (or other school associate) administers the test, reading the directions.
- Please check with your school/testing site regarding its testing procedures, as these may differ.

## COGAT® LEVEL 7 FORMAT

- Students in first grade take the COGAT® Level 7.
- The Quantitative (Math) Battery has 44 questions.
- The test is divided into 3 main parts, each called a "Battery." Each Battery has three question types. See the chart below.

| VERBAL BATTERY | NON-VERBAL BATTERY | QUANTITATIVE BATTERY |
|---|---|---|
| Picture Analogies: 16 Questions | Figure Analogies: 16 Questions | Number Analogies: 16 Questions |
| Picture Classification: 16 Questions | Figure Classification: 16 Questions | Number Puzzles: 12 Questions |
| Sentence Completion: 16 Questions | Paper Folding: 12 Questions | Number Patterns: 16 Questions |

- Often, schools administer one Battery per day, allowing approximately 45 minutes per Battery.
- Students have around 15 minutes to complete each question type (for example, students would have around 15 minutes to complete Figure Analogies).
- See the following pages for examples and explanations of each question type.

## COGAT® SCORING

- Students receive points for correct answers. Points are not deducted for incorrect answers. (Therefore, students should at least guess versus leaving a question blank.)
- In general, schools have a "cut-off" COGAT® score, which they consider together with additional criteria, for gifted & talented acceptance. This varies by school.
- This score is usually at least 98%. (However, some schools accept scores of 95% or even 85%.)
- A score of 98% means that your child scored as well as, or better than, 98% of those in his/her testing group.
- COGAT® scores are available for the entire test and can be broken down by Battery.
- Depending on the school/program, such a "cut-off" score may only be required on one or two of the Batteries (and not on the test overall).
- It is essential to check with your school/program for their acceptance procedures.
- The COGAT® Practice Tests in this book can not yield these percentiles because they have not been given to a large enough group of students to produce an accurate comparison/calculation.

# HOW TO USE THIS BOOK

1. Go over the Question Examples together with your child. These begin on the next page.

2. Do Practice Test 1 (Workbook Format)
   - Do these questions with your child, especially if this is your child's first exposure to COGAT®-prep questions. These questions have a "workbook format," meaning they are meant to be done together.
   - Do not assign a time limit.
   - Talk about what the question is asking your child to do.
   - Questions progress in difficulty. (The first few questions are quite simple.)
   - Go over the answers using the Answer Key.
   - For questions missed, go over the answers again, discussing what makes the correct answer better than the other choices.

3. Do the remaining Practice Tests following Practice Test 1.
   - If your child progressed easily through Practice Test 1, see how well they can do without your help.
   - If your child needed assistance with much of Practice Test 1, then continue to assist your child with Practice Test 2.
   - If you wish to assign a time limit, assign around 15 minutes per question type.
   - Go over the answers using the Answer Key.
   - For questions missed, go over the answers again, discussing what makes the correct answer better than the other choices.

4. **Need more practice?**

   - **Help your child ace the test!**

   - **Check out Savant Test Prep™ books on Amazon®.**

# TEST-TAKING TIPS

- Ensure your child listens carefully to the directions.
- Make sure (s)he does not rush through questions. (There is no prize for finishing first!) Tell your child to look carefully at the question. Then, tell your child to look at each answer choice before marking his/her answer.
  - If you notice your child continuing to rush through the questions, tell him/her to point to each part of the question. Then, point to each answer choice.
- If (s)he does not know the answer, then use the process of elimination. Cross out any answer choices which are clearly incorrect, then choose from those remaining.
- This tip/suggestion is entirely at your discretion. You may wish to offer some sort of special motivation to encourage your child to do his/her best. An extra incentive of, for example, an art set, a building block set, or a special outing can go a long way in motivating young learners!
- The night before testing, make sure your child has enough sleep, without any interruptions. (Think about the difference in **your** brain function with a good night's sleep vs. without. The same goes for your child's.)
- The morning before the test, ensure your child eats a healthy breakfast with protein and complex carbs. Do not let them eat sugar, chocolate, etc.
- If you can choose the time your child will take the test (for example, if (s)he will take the test individually, instead of at school with a group), opt for a morning testing session, when your child will be most alert.

# QUESTION EXAMPLES

- Here is an overview of the COGAT® question types.
- This section has <u>simple</u> examples, to introduce your child to test concepts.
    - Do these examples together with your child.
- Below the questions are explanations for parents.

## 1. NUMBER ANALOGIES (QUANTITATIVE BATTERY)

**• Directions (read to child):** The pictures in the top boxes go together in some way. Look at the bottom boxes. One box is empty. Look at the row of answer choices next to the boxes. Which one of these choices goes with the picture in the bottom box like the pictures in the top box go together?

**• Explanation (read to child):** In the left box, there are 7 objects (stars). In the right box, there are 2 objects. From left to right, we see that 5 objects have been taken away. So, the rule here is "5 are taken away" or "-5." In the bottom left box, there are 9 objects. If our rule is "5 are taken away," then if you have 9 and you take away 5, you get 4. The third answer choice is correct.

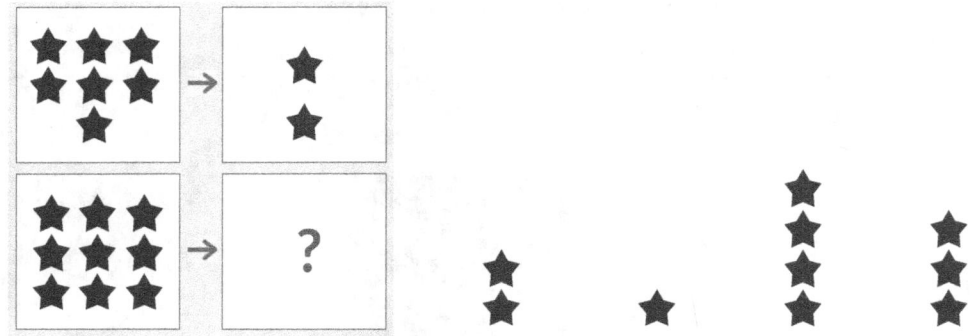

**•Tip:** Some analogies involve addition and subtraction, while others require children to do more complex calculations: dividing in half, doubling, or tripling. If your child first tries to add or subtract, but no answer choice matches the "rule," then try to double or triple (if the number increases from left to right) or try to halve (if the number decreases from left to right).

**• Show your child the example below.**

**• Explanation (read to child):** In the top left box, there are 2 stars. In the top right box, there is 1 star. Let's try the rule "take away 1." In the bottom left box, there are 4 stars. If our rule is "take away 1," then the answer should be 3 stars. However, there isn't an answer choice with 3 stars. Let's look again at the top boxes. If you divide 2 in half, you get 1. Let's try the rule "divide in half." If you take the 4 stars in the bottom left box and divide them in half, you get 2. The choice with two stars is correct.

## 2. NUMBER PUZZLES (QUANTITATIVE BATTERY)

• **Directions (read to child):** Which train car should you choose so that the top train is carrying the same number of items as the bottom train?

• **Explanation (read to child):** The top train carries four items (four hearts). The bottom train carries two items. Next to the train car with two hearts is a train car with a question mark. Which train car from the answer choices should be put here so that the bottom train would have the same number of items (hearts) as the top train? It would be the choice with 2 hearts (choice B).

• **Explanation for the below question (read to child):** Look at the top train and count the number of items in the train. The top train has 5 items (5 triangles). Look at the bottom train and count the number of items. The bottom train has 6 items. Like the earlier questions, we need to figure out which train car from the answer choices would be put in the place of the train car with a question mark. Like the earlier questions, the top train and the bottom train must carry the same number of items. For the top train and the bottom train to do this, one triangle must be taken away from the bottom train. In the answer choices, if an item has an "X" on it, this means that it would be taken away from the train. We need to take away one triangle, so we need to choose the train car with one "X" on top of the item. The last choice shows this.

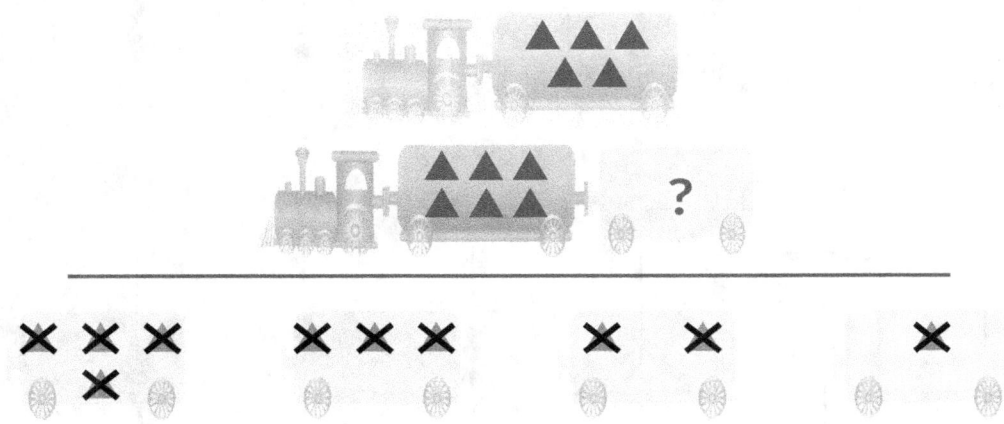

7

## 3. NUMBER PATTERNS (QUANTITATIVE BATTERY)

• **Directions (read to child):** Which rod should go in the place of the missing rod to finish the pattern?

• **Explanation for #1 (read to child):** Before the missing rod, the other rods have made a pattern that we need to figure out. Then, we will complete the pattern with the correct answer choice. From left to right, we see that the pattern is: 1 - 2 - 1 - 2 - 1. After 1, comes 2. This means that the missing rod needs 2 beads.

• Make sure your child accurately counts the number of beads. In the examples below, there are numbers under the rods indicating the number of beads. The practice test questions do not have these numbers.

• After you do #1, go over questions #2 - #7 together. The pattern and the answer are already given.

1.

Pattern: the number of beads decreases by 1. The answer is 1.

2.
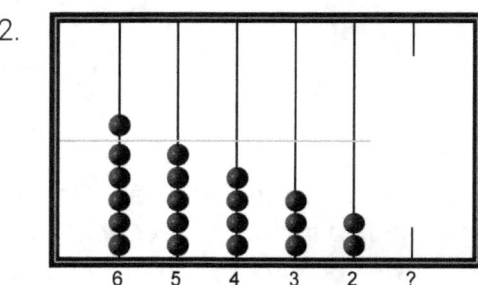  

Pattern: every other rod increases by 1. And, the alternate rods equal 0. The answer is 0.

3.
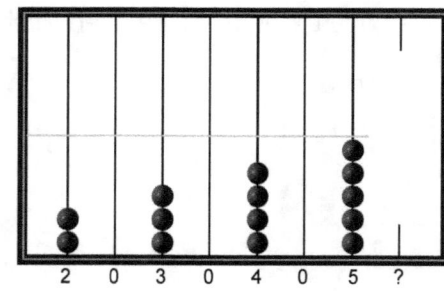  

Pattern: the rods repeat 7 - 5 - 3. The answer is 7.

4.
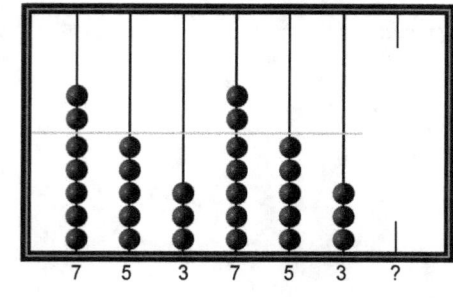  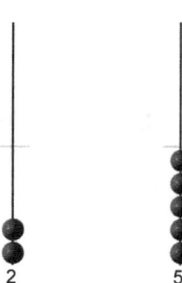

8

This one may be challenging. Every other rod increases by one (1 - 2 - 3 - 4). Then, every other rod (the alternate rods), increases by one (4 - 5 - 6 - 7). With the alternating rods increasing 1, 2, 3, 4, this means that the next rod will be 5.

5.

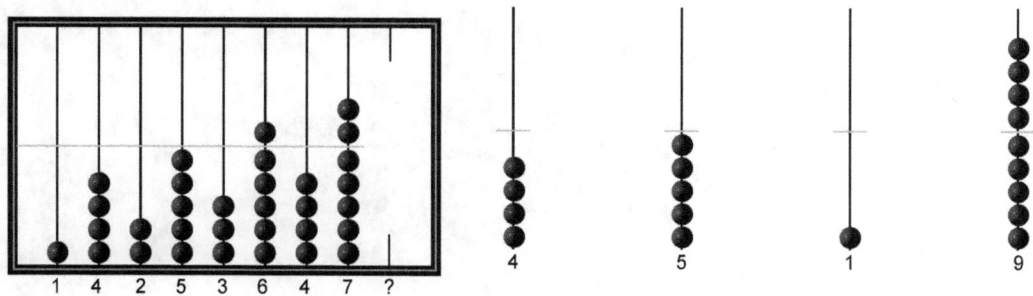

This one may be challenging also. Every other rod decreases by one (5 - 4 - 3). Then, every other rod (the alternate rods), increase by one (1 - 2 - 3). With the alternating rods decreasing 5, 4, 3, this means that the next rod will be 2.

6.

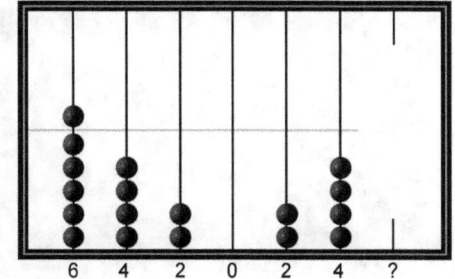    

Pattern: the rods decrease with the pattern 6 - 4 - 2, then increase with the reverse pattern 2 - 4 - 6.

7.

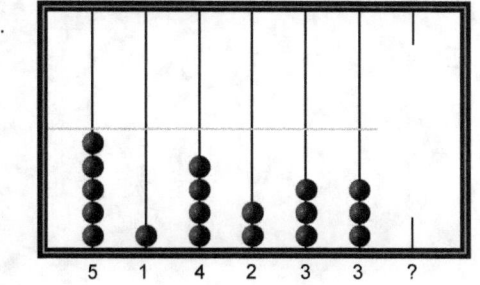    

**Practice Test 1 (Workbook Format) begins on the next page.**

COGAT® Practice Test 1
(Workbook Format) -

# NUMBER ANALOGIES

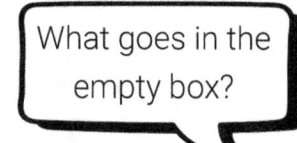

Sara

**Explanation (for parents):** A more detailed explanation of Math Analogies is on p.6. Look over p.6, if you have not already. Your child must figure out how the images in the top set of boxes are related mathematically. Then, (s)he must figure out which answer choice would go with the bottom left image so that the bottom set would have the same relationship. After counting the objects in the boxes, you may want your child to write the number by the box, so (s)he does not forget the quantity.

**Directions for the example:** Look at the top box on the left. There are 3 suns. Look at the top box on the right. There is 1 sun. What has changed from the picture on the left to the one on the right? We need to come up with a "rule" to describe what has happened. The right box will have 2 less than the left box. Next, let's look carefully at the bottom row. What do you see in the left box? There are 5 clouds. Look at the right box. It is empty. Look carefully at the row of pictures next to the boxes. These are the answer choices. Which one of these goes in the empty box? Remember, our rule is that the right box will have 2 less than the left box. If the left box has 5 clouds, and our rule is that the right box will have 2 less, then that means 3 clouds is the answer. Choice B has 3 clouds.

**Directions for the rest:** Which answer choice would go inside the empty box at the bottom?

1.

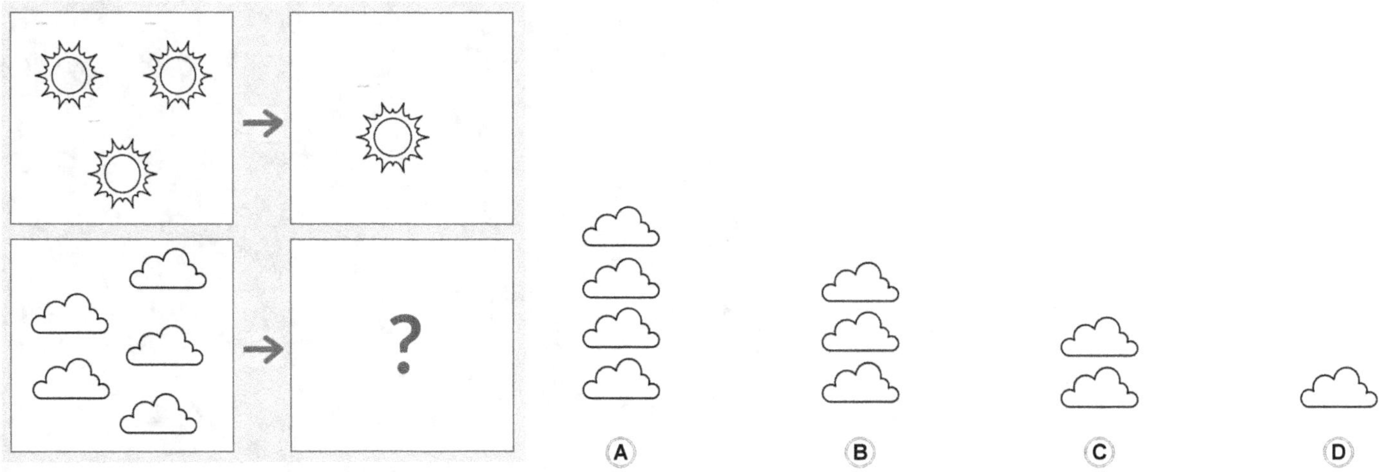

A   B   C   D

2.

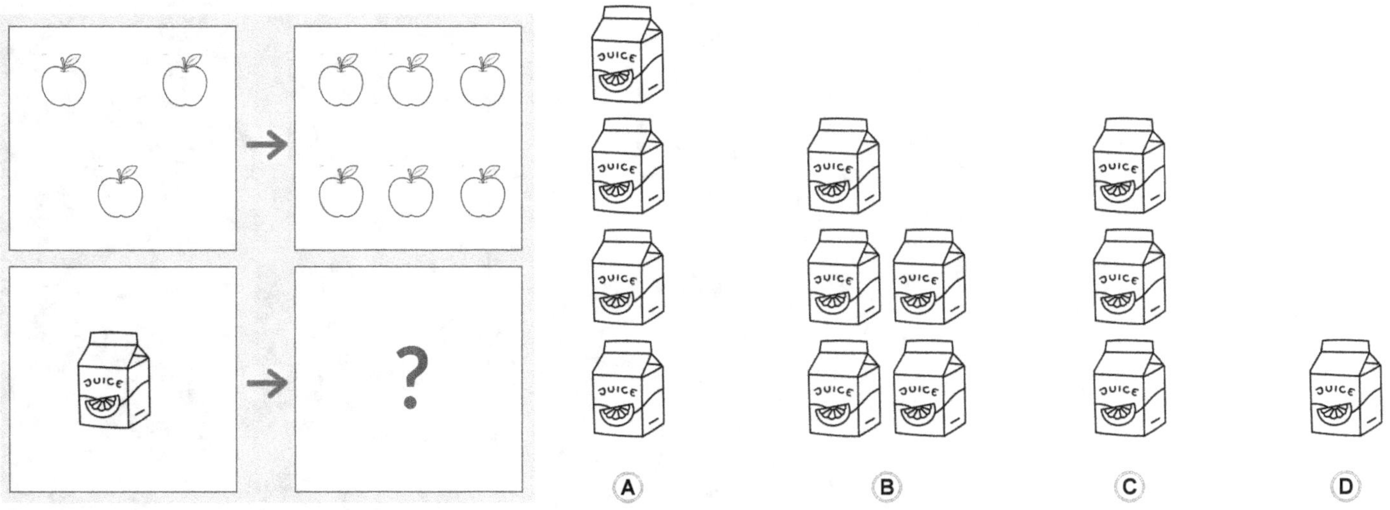

A   B   C   D

3.

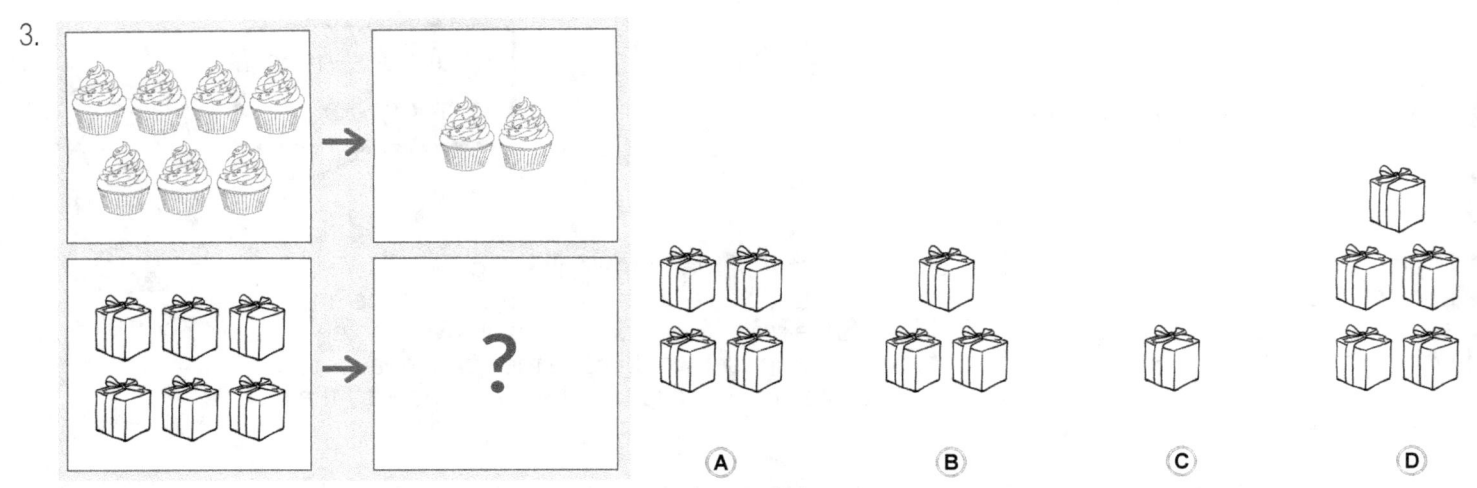

A     B     C     D

4.

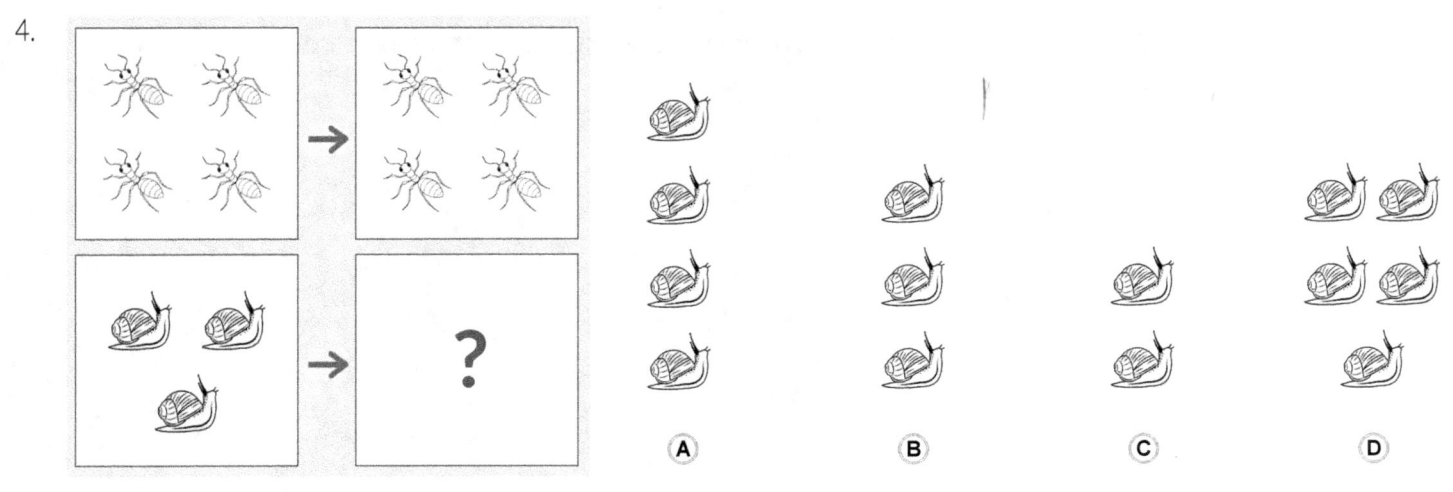

A     B     C     D

5.

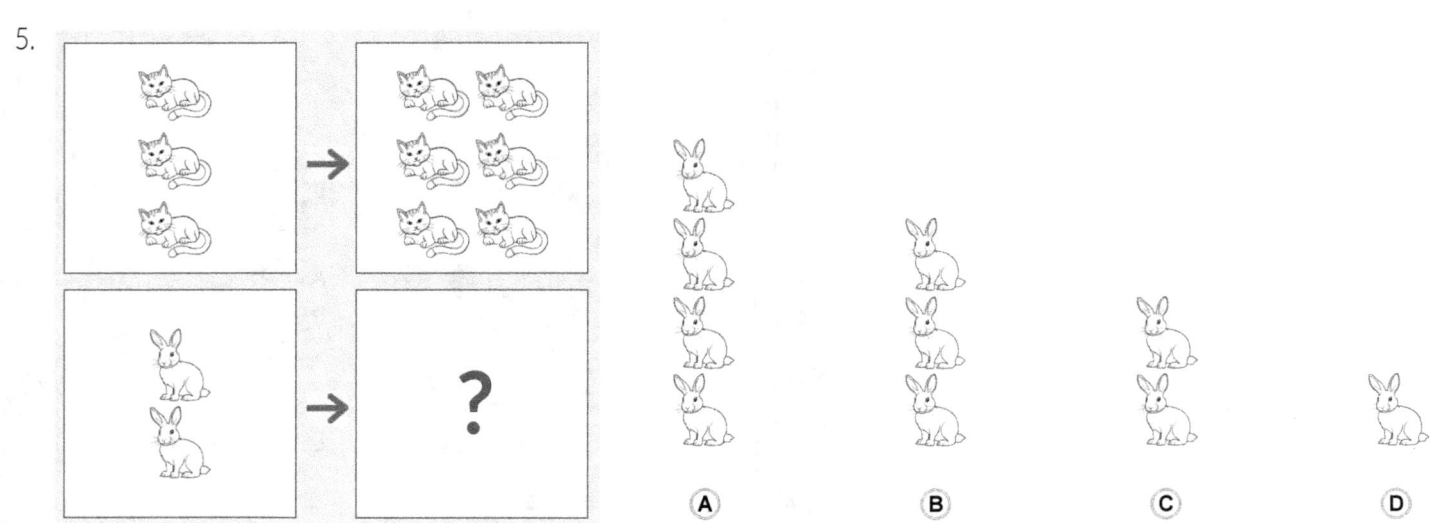

A     B     C     D

6.

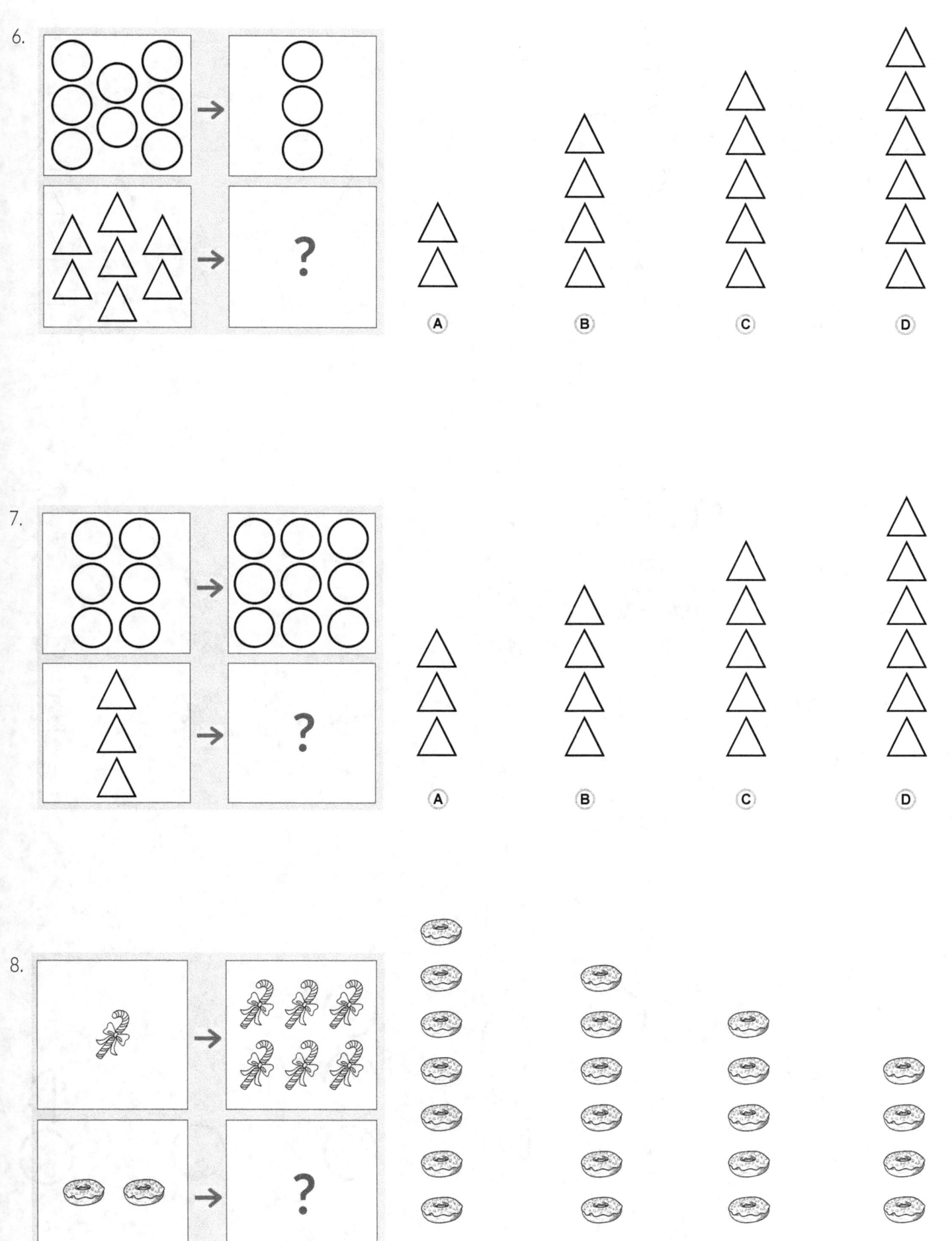

(A) (B) (C) (D)

7.

(A) (B) (C) (D)

8.

(A) (B) (C) (D)

13

9.

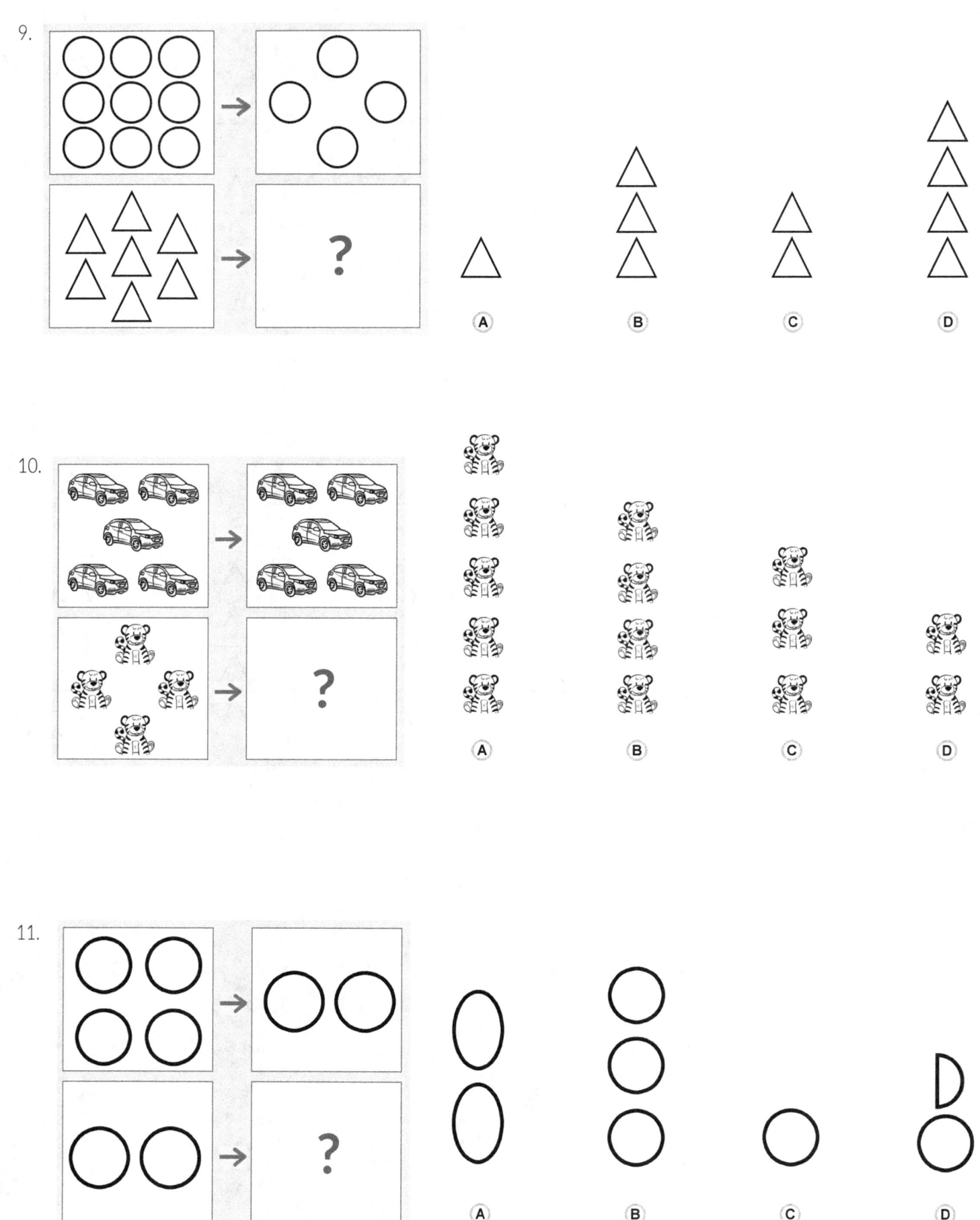

10.

11.

14

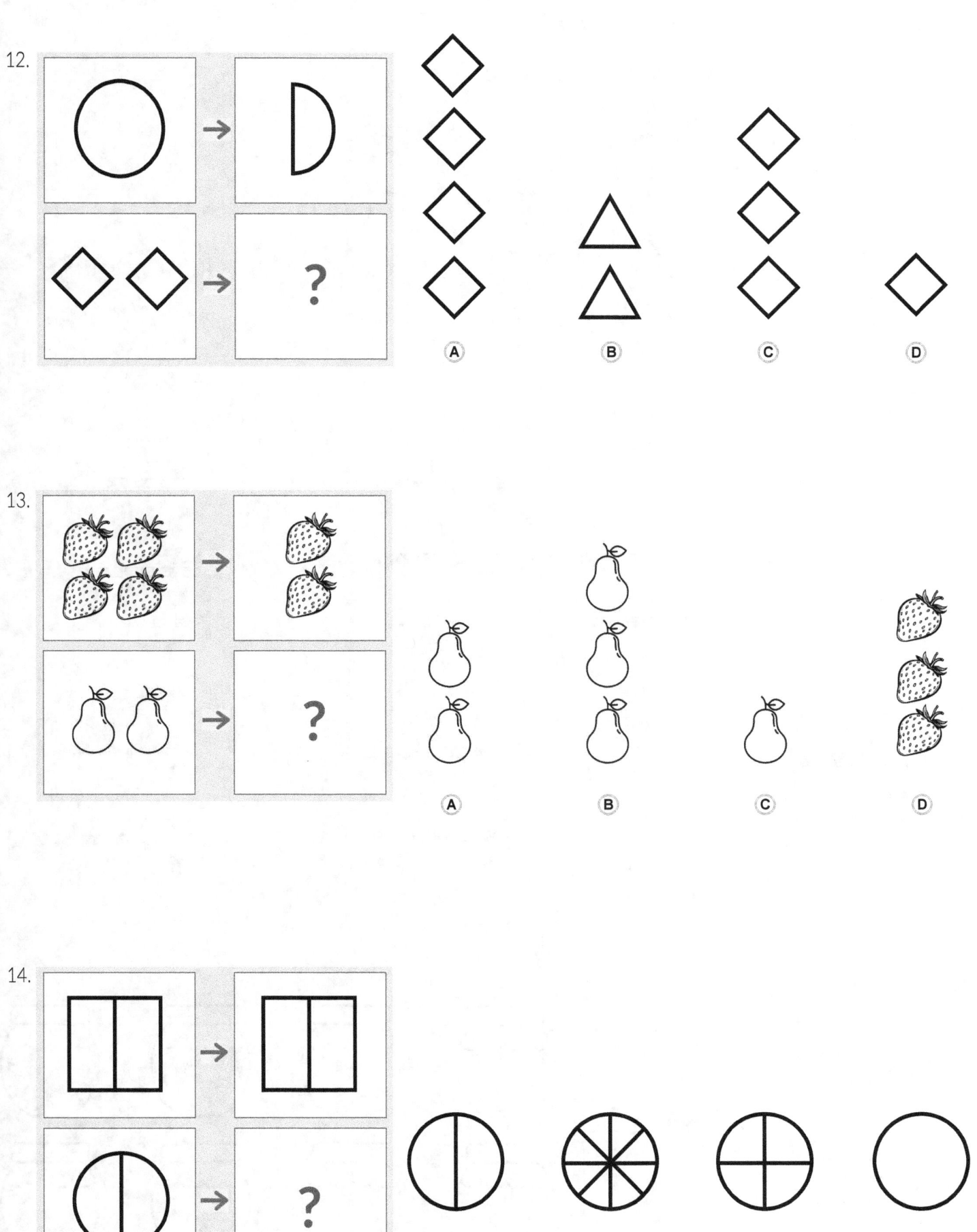

12.

13.

14.

15

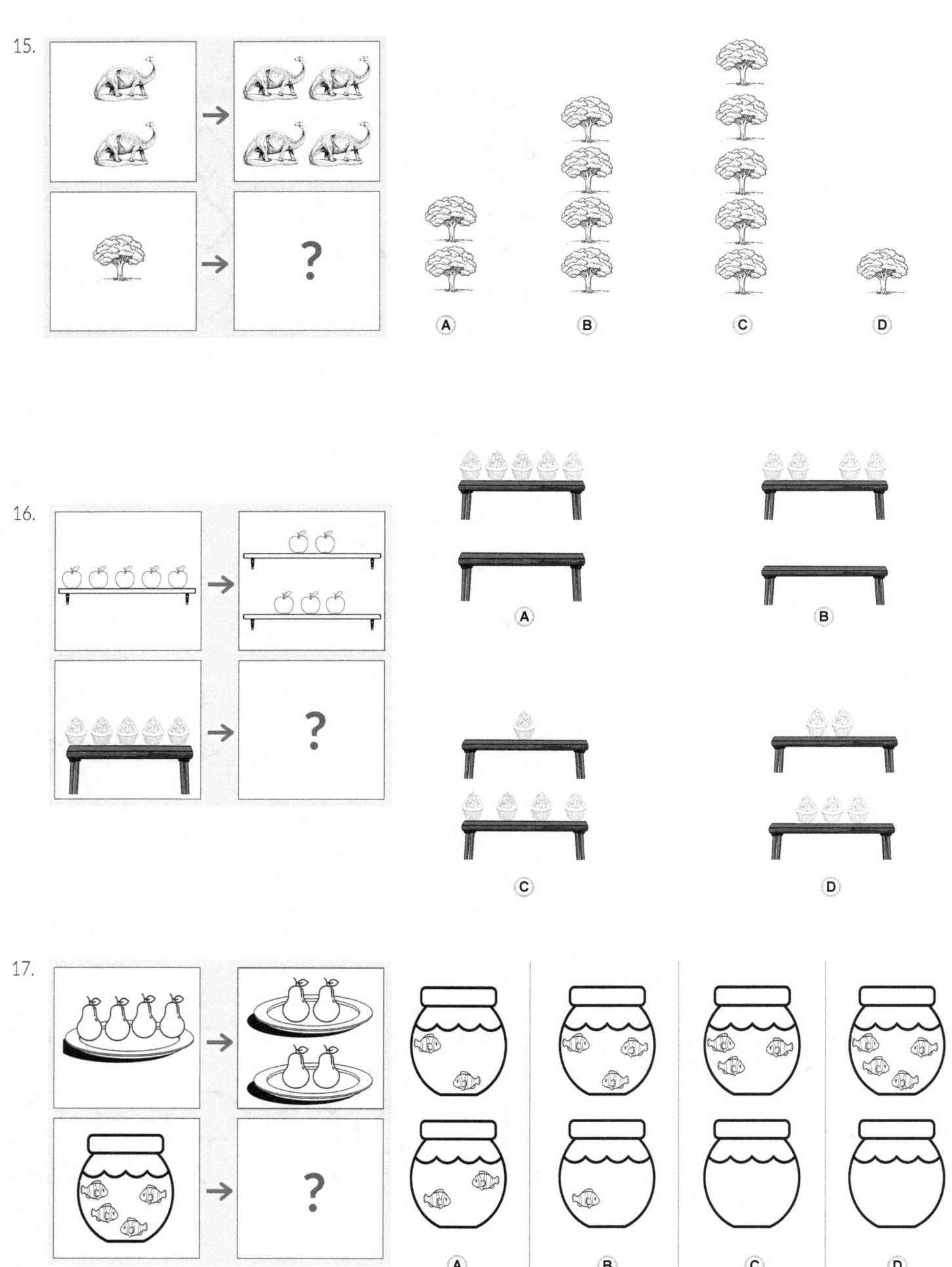

15.

16.

17.

16

# NUMBER PUZZLES

## "Which train car makes the top and bottom the same?" Kai asks.

Kai

**Directions for Question #1 (read to child):** Look at the top train. Let's count the number of things it's carrying inside the train cars. It is carrying 6 gray circles. Look at the bottom train. The bottom train has 3 circles inside the left train car. The right train car has a question mark. We must figure out which train car in the answer choices would go in place of the train car with the question mark so that the top train and the bottom train have the same number of gray circles inside. Remember that the top train has 6 gray circles. So, the bottom train car on the right must have 3 gray circles. Three plus three equals 6. Which answer choice has 3 gray circles? Choice B is the answer. (**Note:** If you haven't gone over p.7 with your child, do so now.)

**Directions for the rest (read to child):** Which train car should you choose so that the top train carries the same number of items as the bottom train?

1.

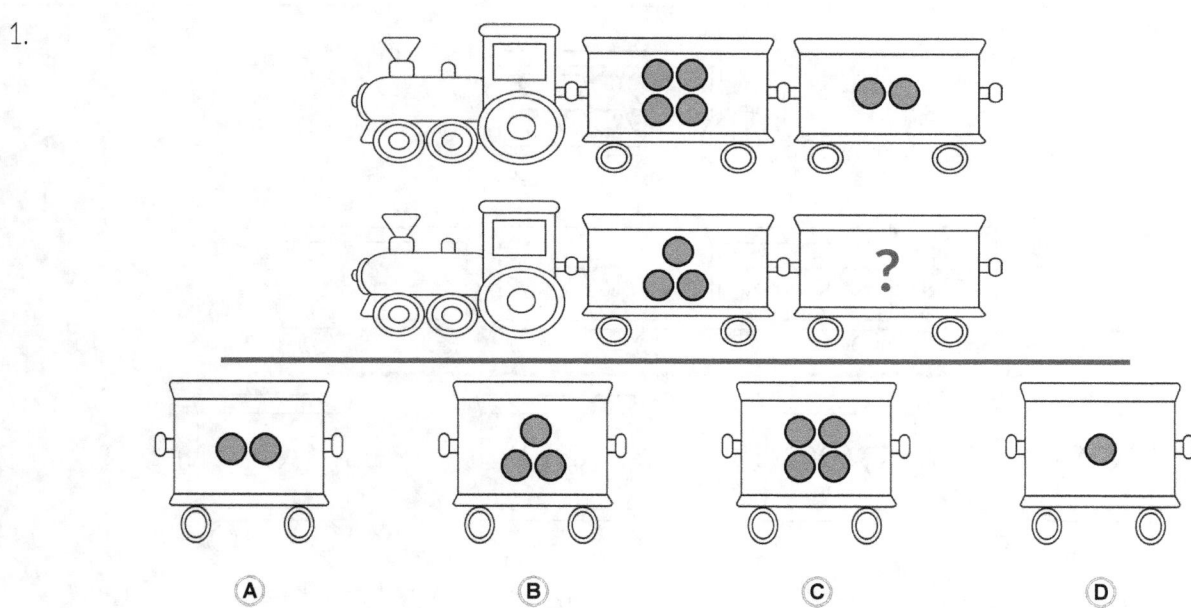

2.

17

3.

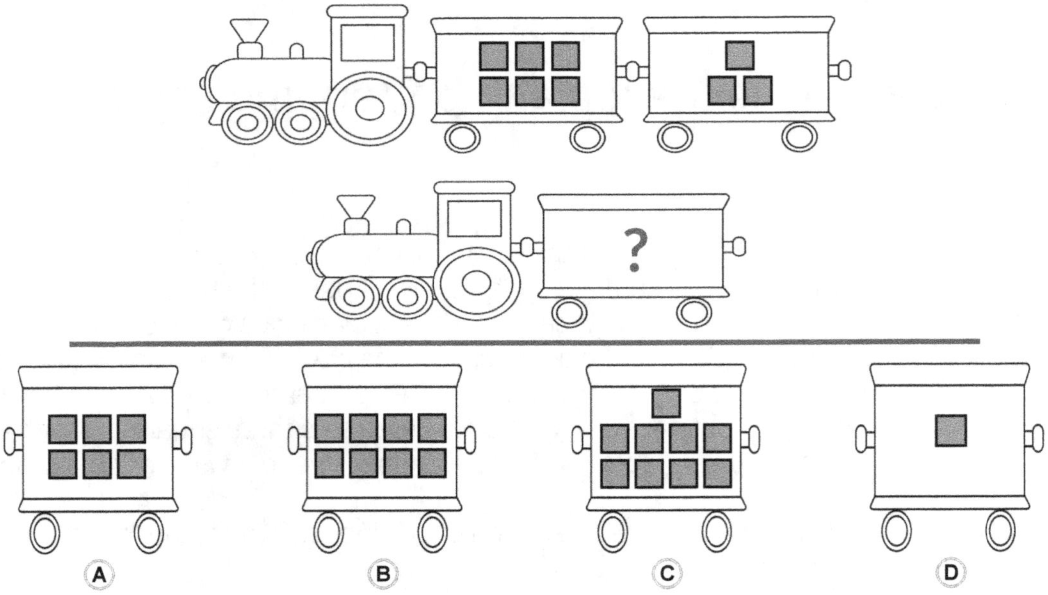

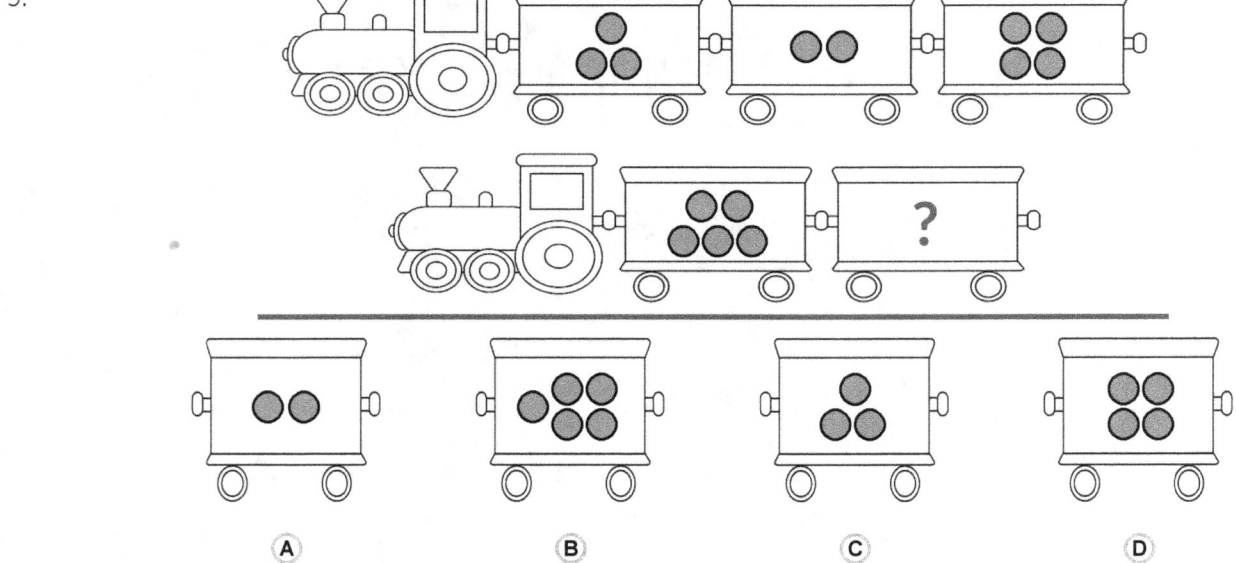

A     B     C     D

4.

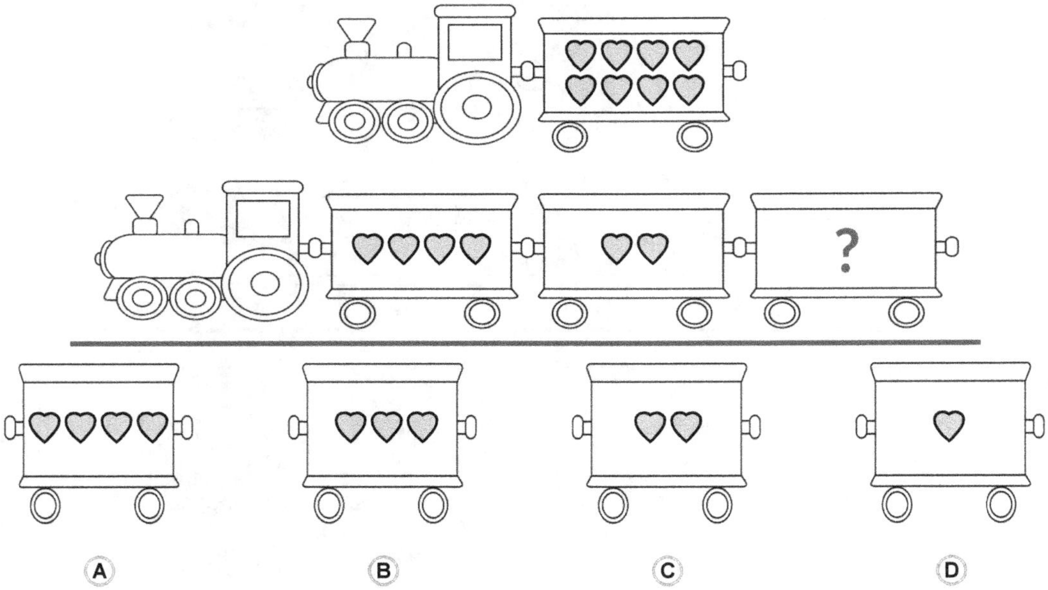

A     B     C     D

5.

A     B     C     D

6.

A          B          C          D

7.

A          B          C          D

8.

A          B          C          D

# NUMBER PUZZLES (subtraction)

• **Explanation for the next questions (read to child):** In the next group of questions, remember that if something has an "X" on it, this means that it would be taken away from the train.

Which train car should you choose so that the top train carries the same number of items as the bottom train?

9.

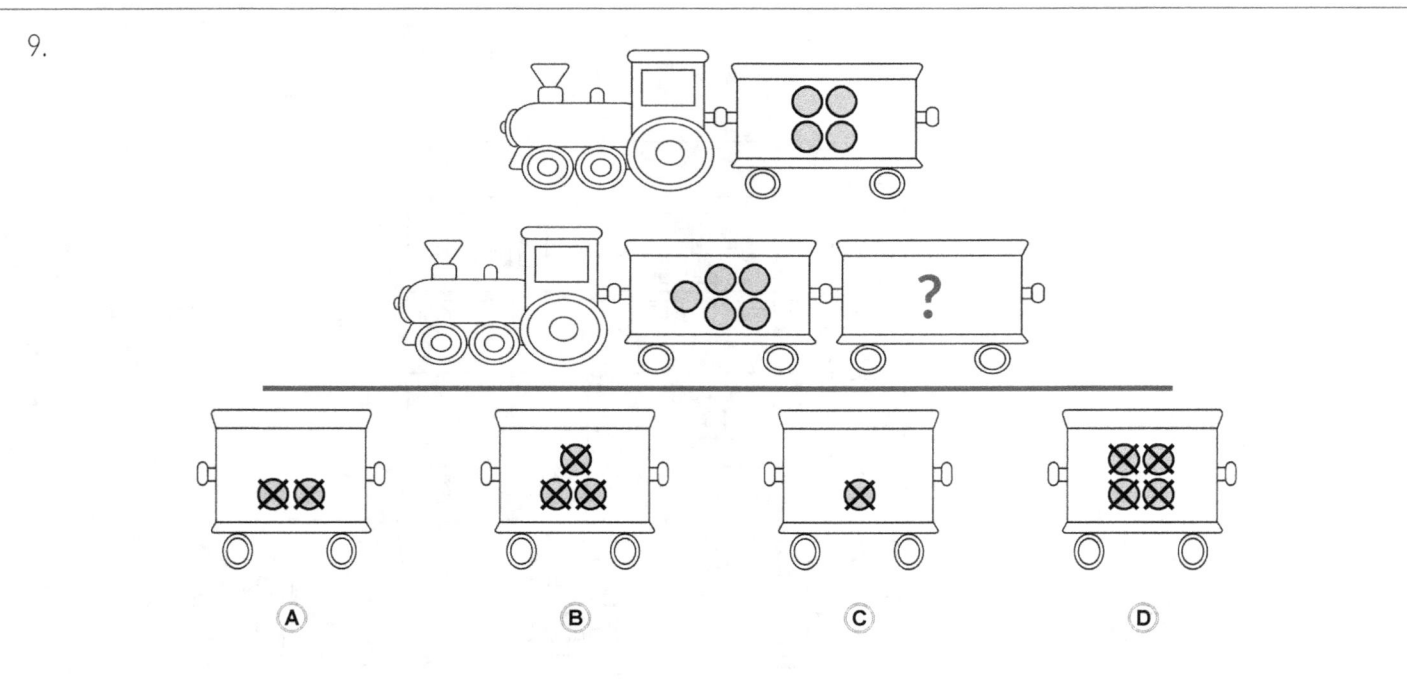

10.

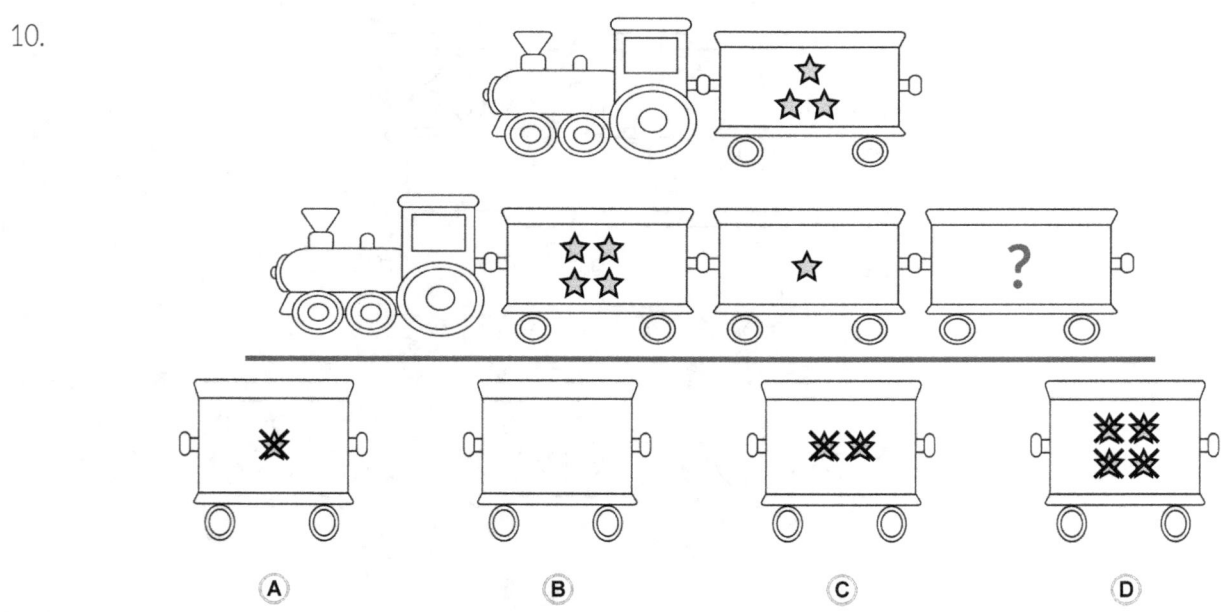

11.

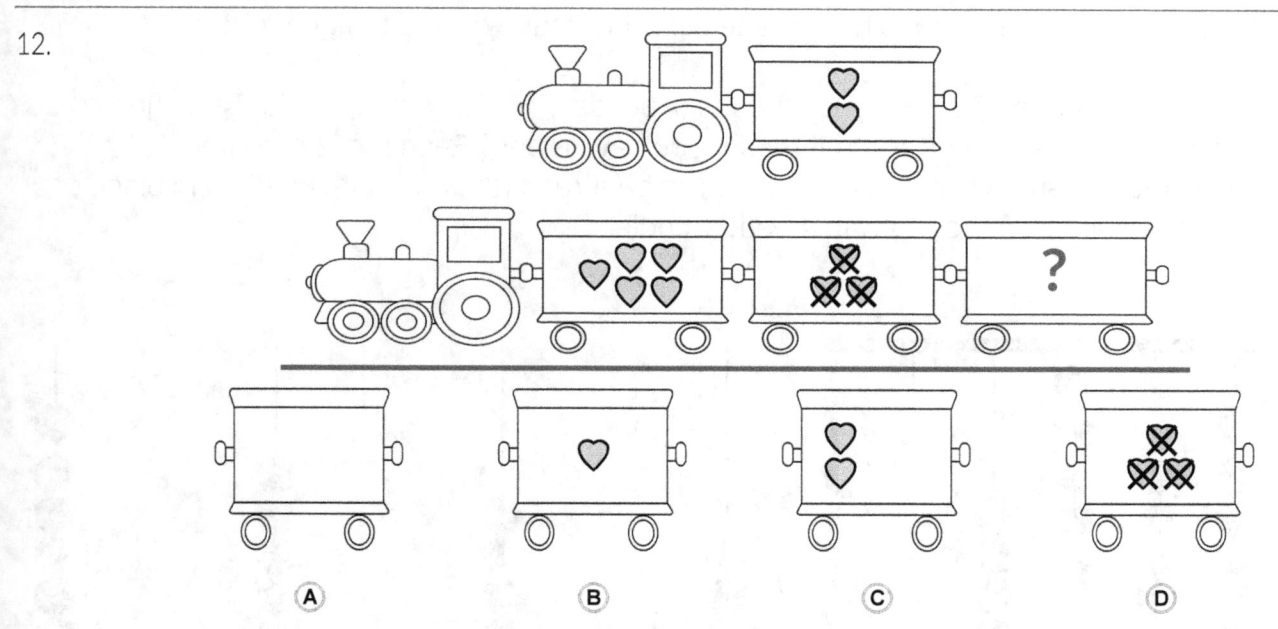

12.

13.

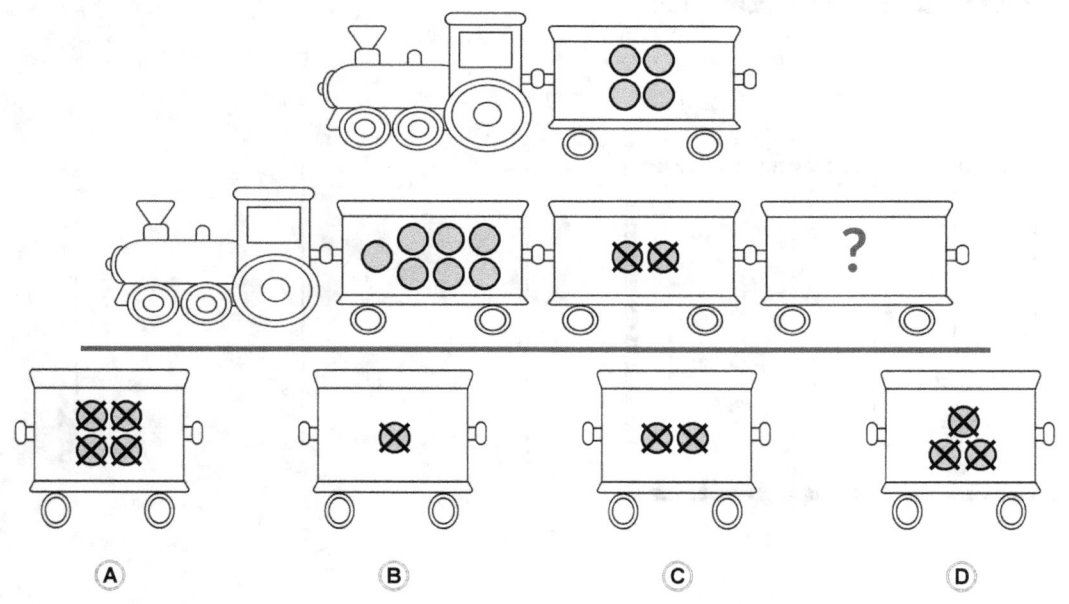

# NUMBER PATTERNS

## "Let's figure out the pattern!" Maya says.

Maya

**Directions (read to child):** Which rod should go in the place of the missing rod to finish the pattern?

**Explanation (for parents):** The final rod of the abacus is missing. Before this missing rod, the rods of the abacus have made a pattern. Your child must look closely to determine the pattern. Go over p.8 with your child, if you haven't already.

Note that some rods do not have any beads. Rods without any beads equal "0". The gray line appears above the 5th bead's place.

**Example (read to child):** The picture below shows an abacus. The abacus has rods going bottom to top. On these rods are beads. These rods have made a pattern that we need to figure out.

First, we see a rod with 6 beads. Then, we see 6 beads, 7 beads, 7 beads, and 4 beads. Then, finally there is a missing rod. What is the pattern that these rods have made? Each rod is repeated: 6, 6, 7, 7, and then 4. If this is the pattern, what should the next rod be after 4 (the rod that would go in place of the missing rod on the abacus)? The rod with 4 beads, choice B.

1.

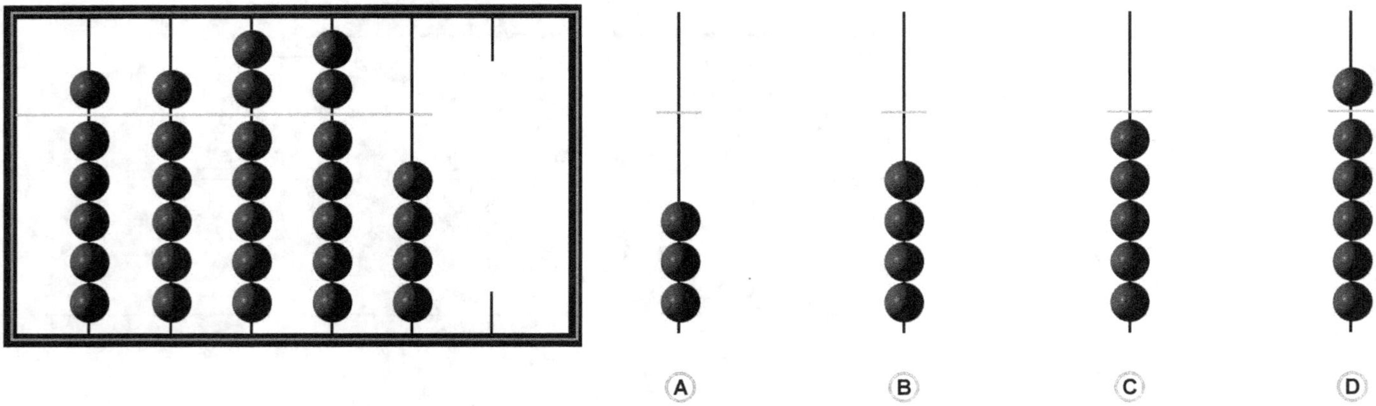

(A)   (B)   (C)   (D)

2.

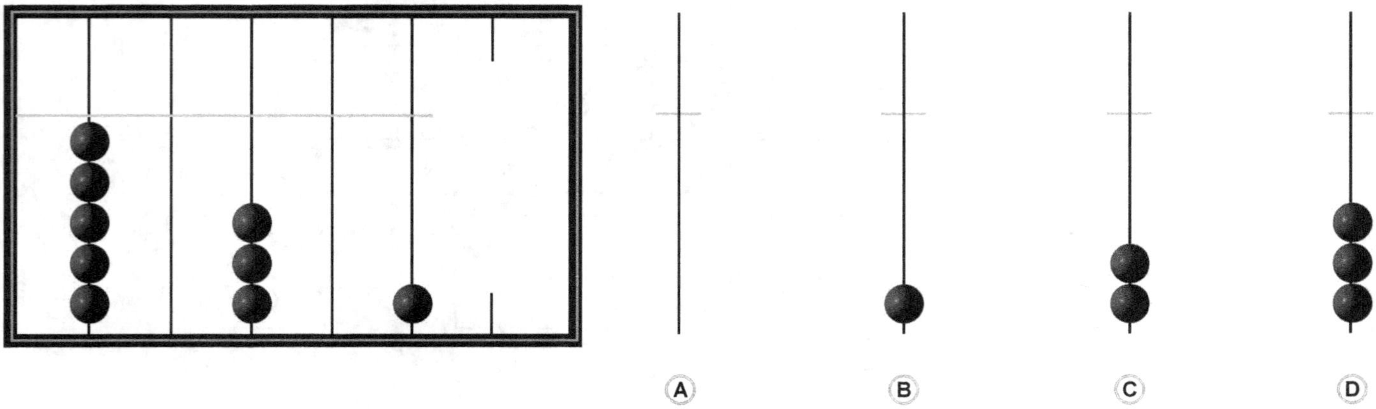

(A)   (B)   (C)   (D)

22

3.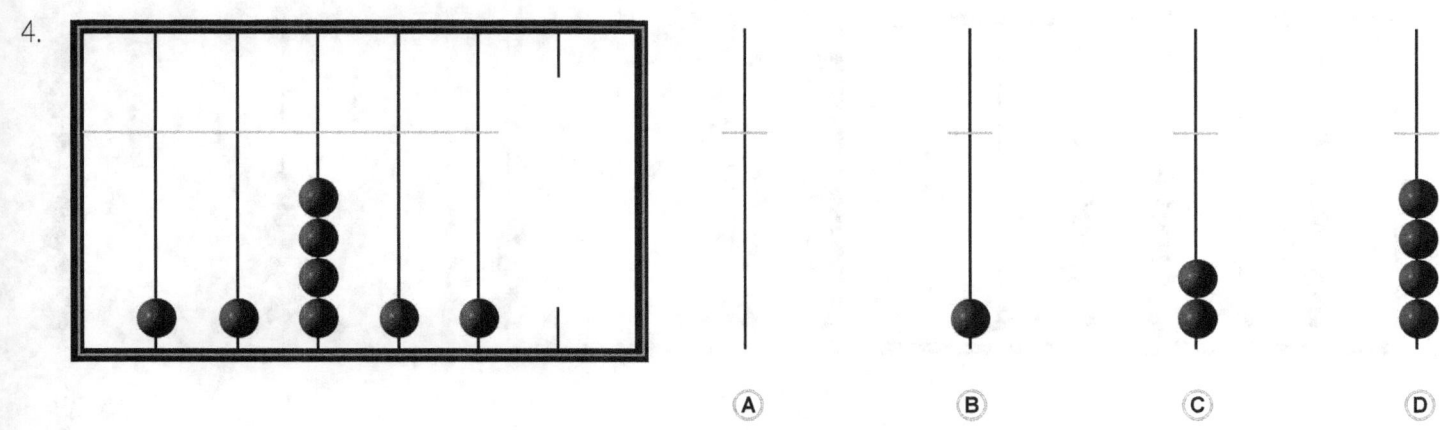

A      B      C      D

4.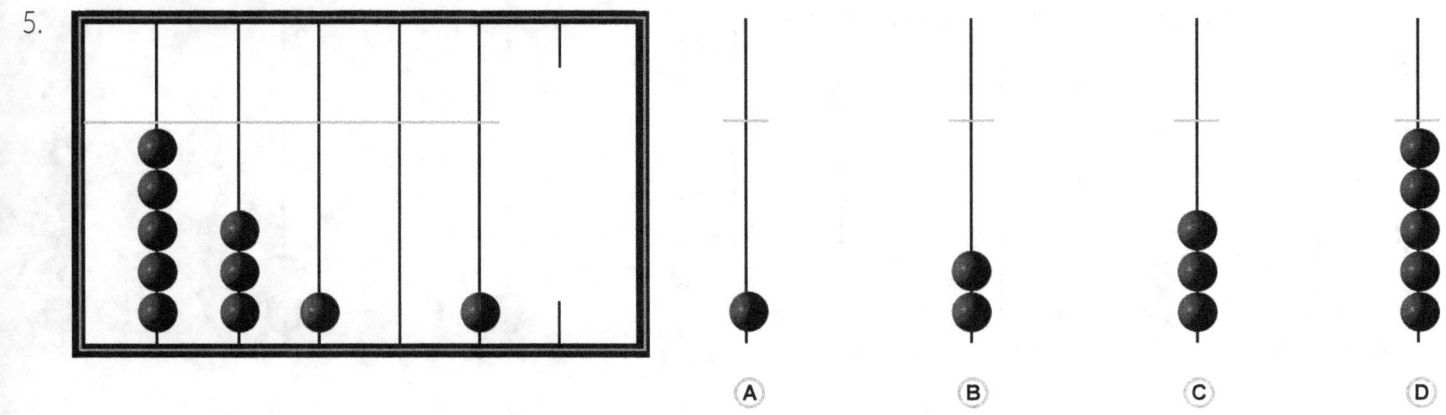

A      B      C      D

5.

A      B      C      D

6.

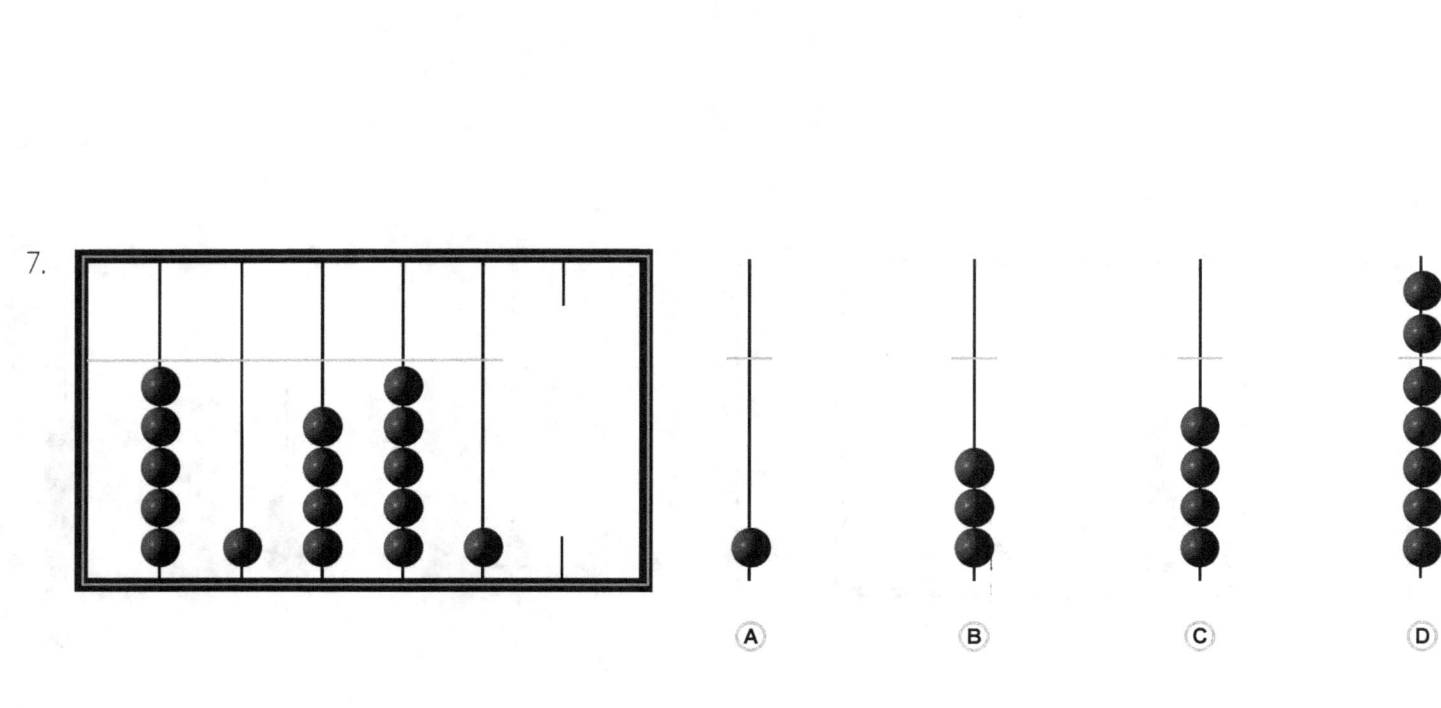

A    B    C    D

7.

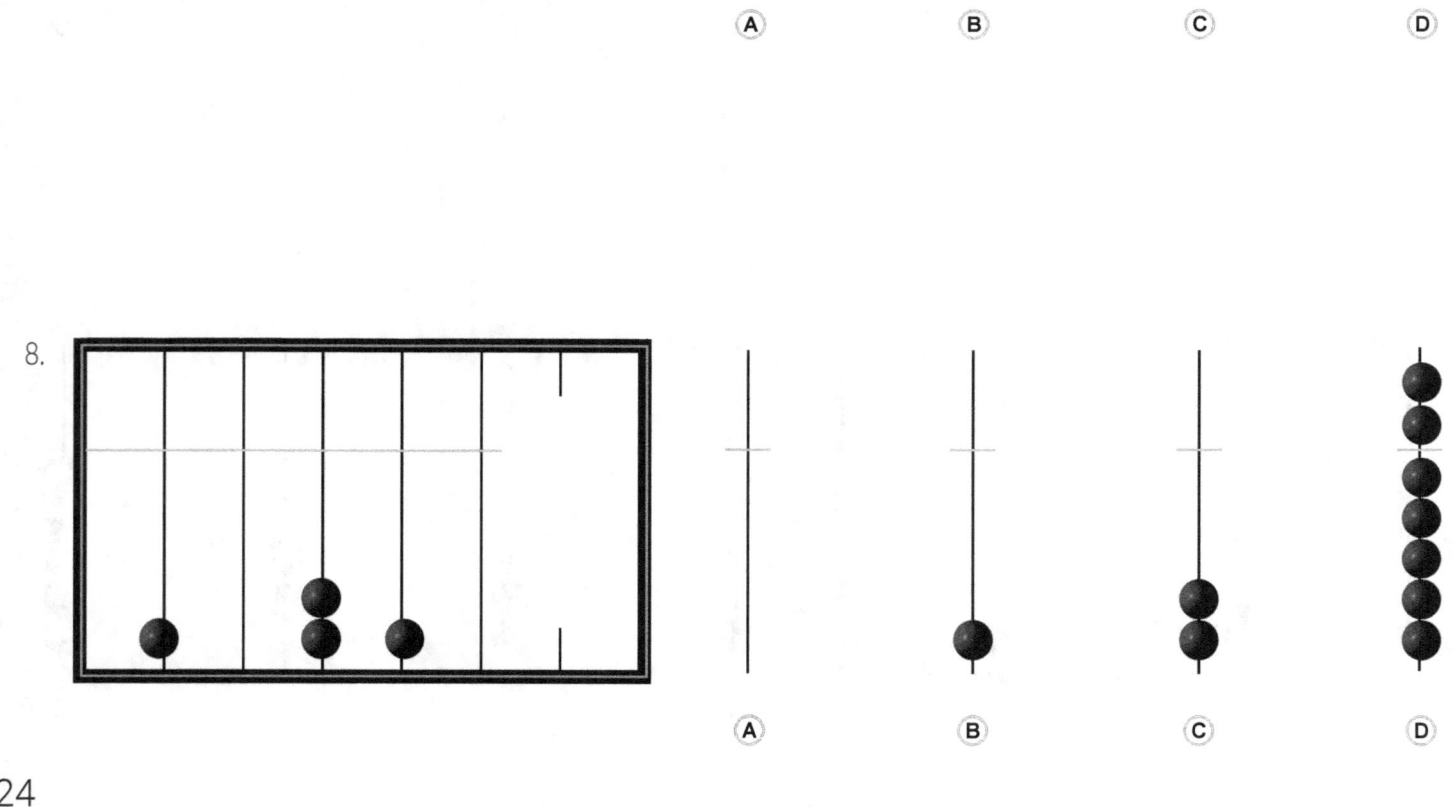

A    B    C    D

8.

A    B    C    D

24

9.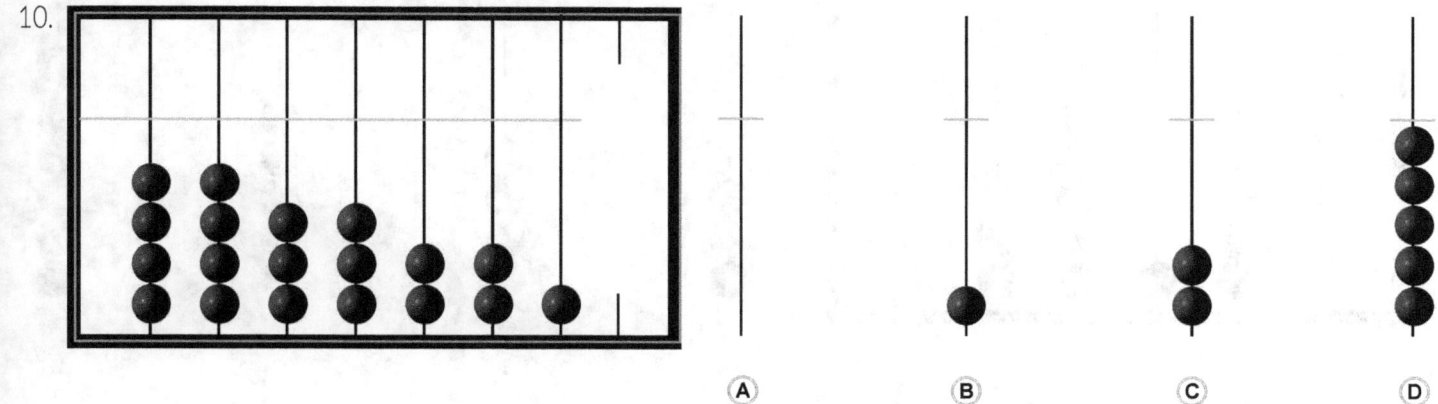

10.

11.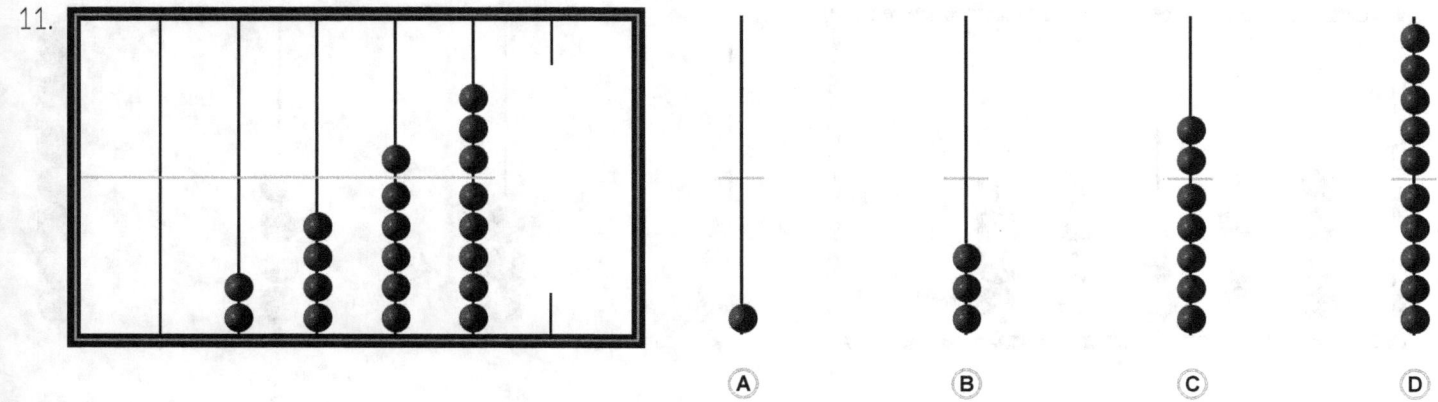

12.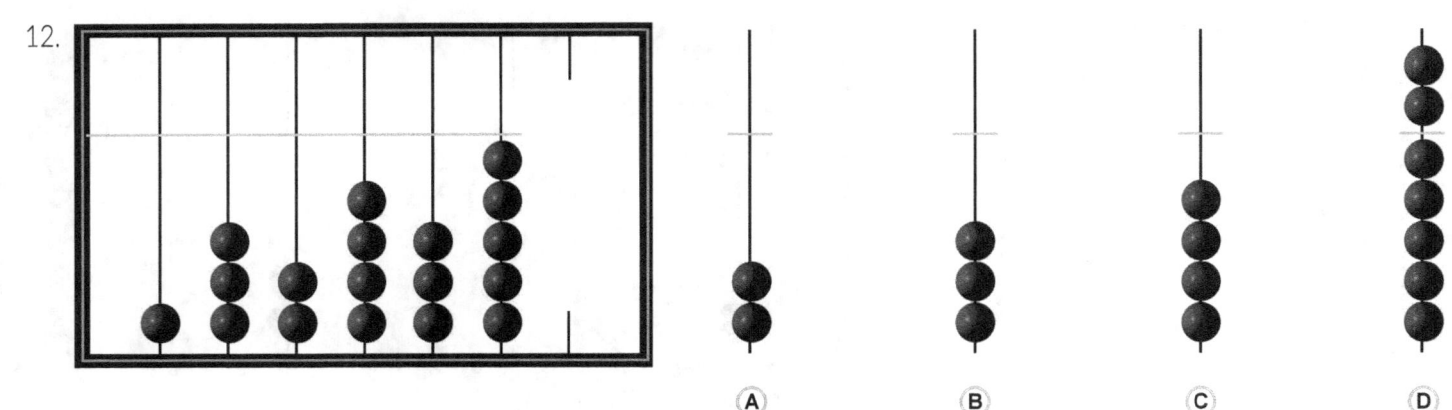

13.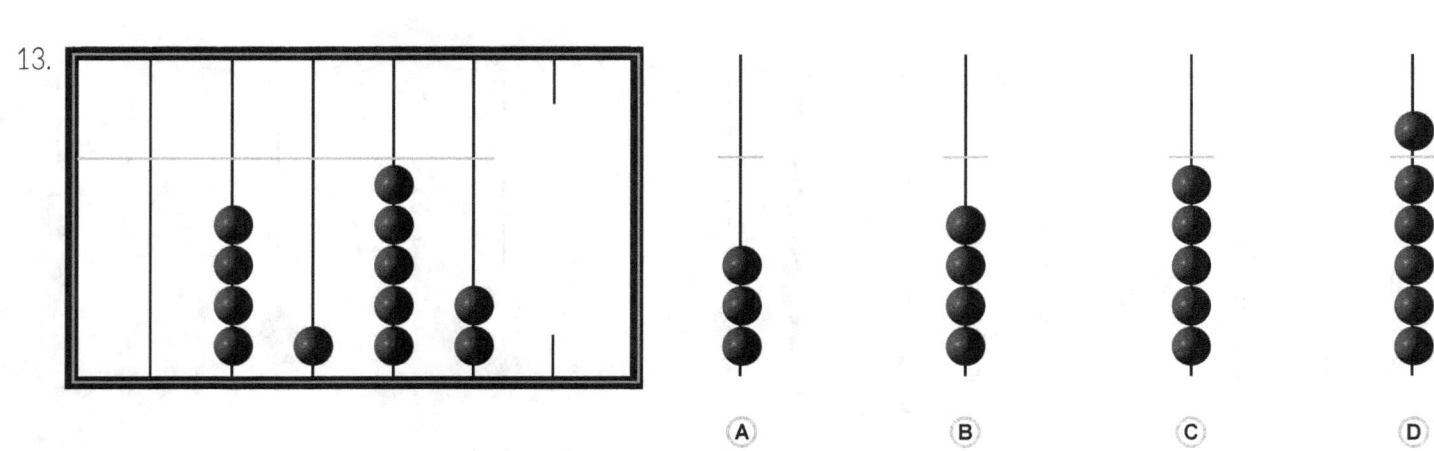

14.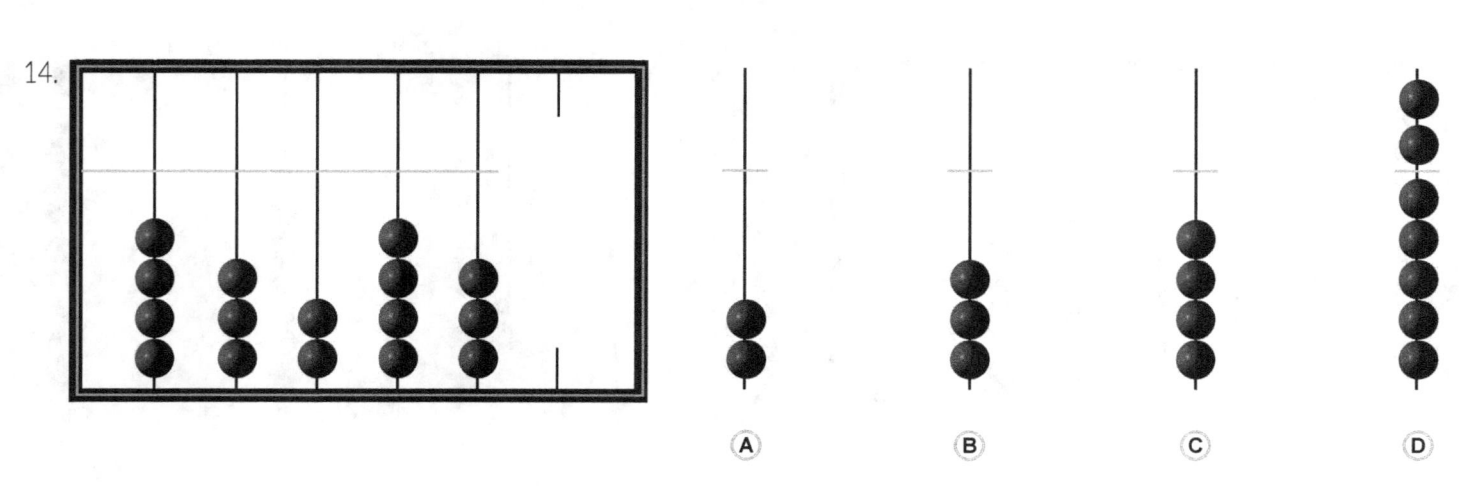

26

15.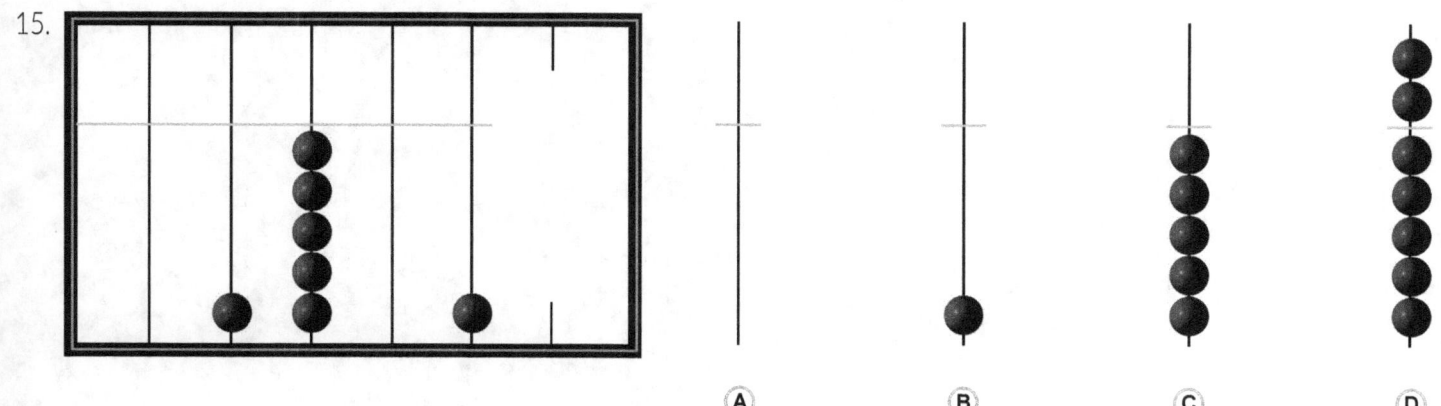

16.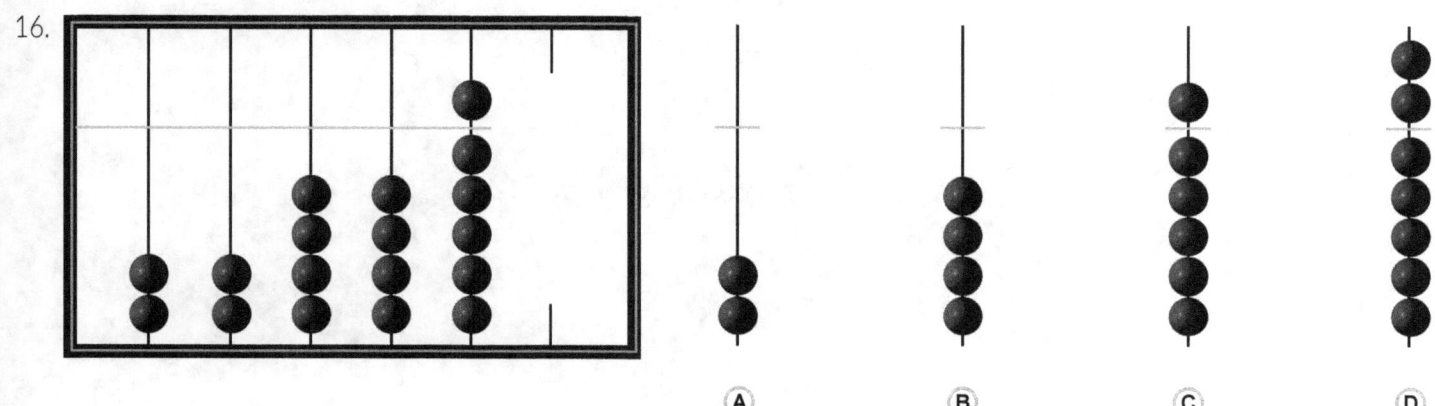

- End of Practice Test 1 (Workbook Format) -

COGAT® Practice Test 2

# START OF PRACTICE TEST 2 / NUMBER ANALOGIES

Directions: The pictures in the top boxes go together in some way. One of the bottom boxes is empty. Which answer choice goes with the picture in the bottom box in the same way the top pictures do?

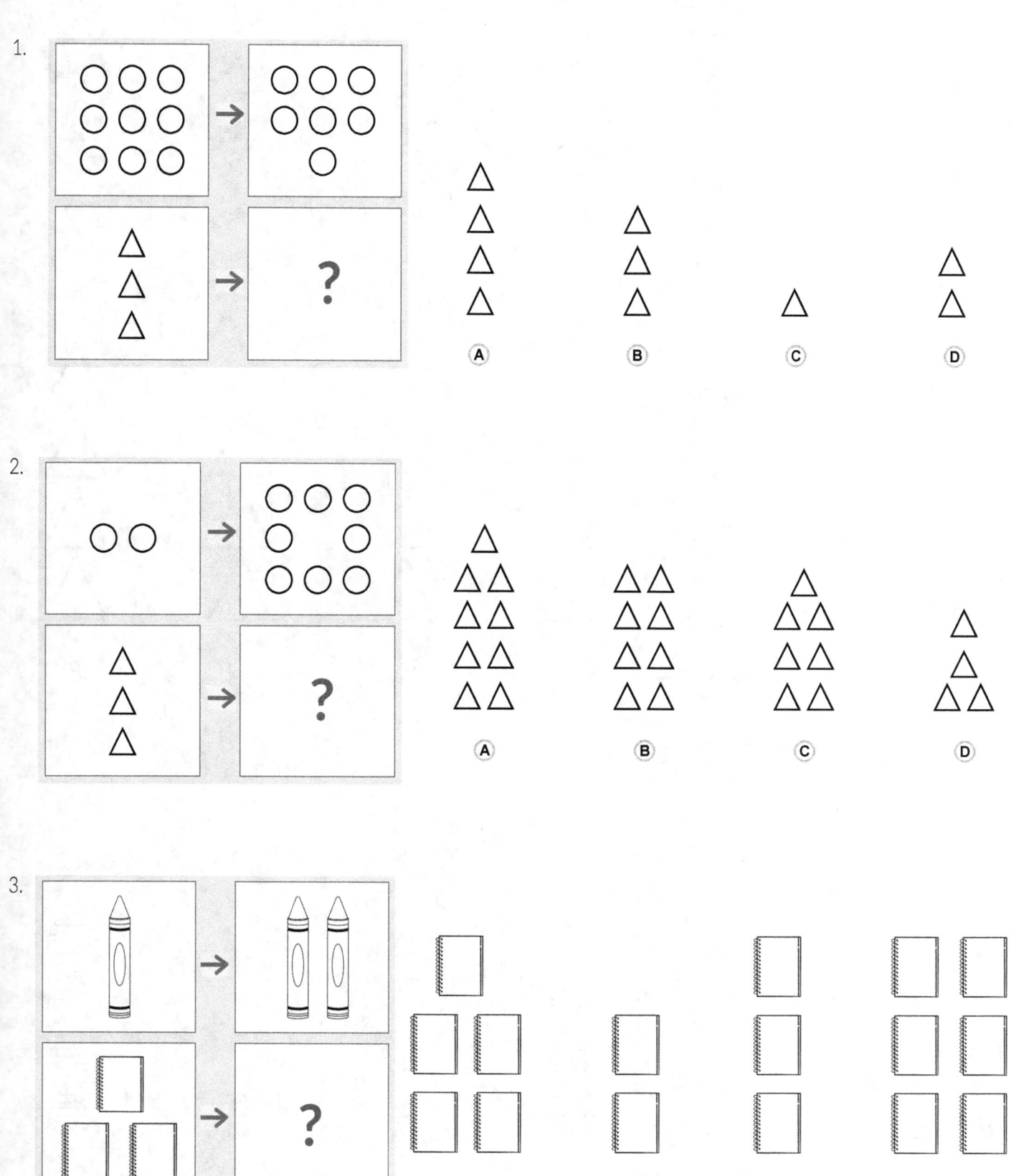

4.

A     B     C     D

5.

A     B     C     D

6.

A     B     C     D

7.

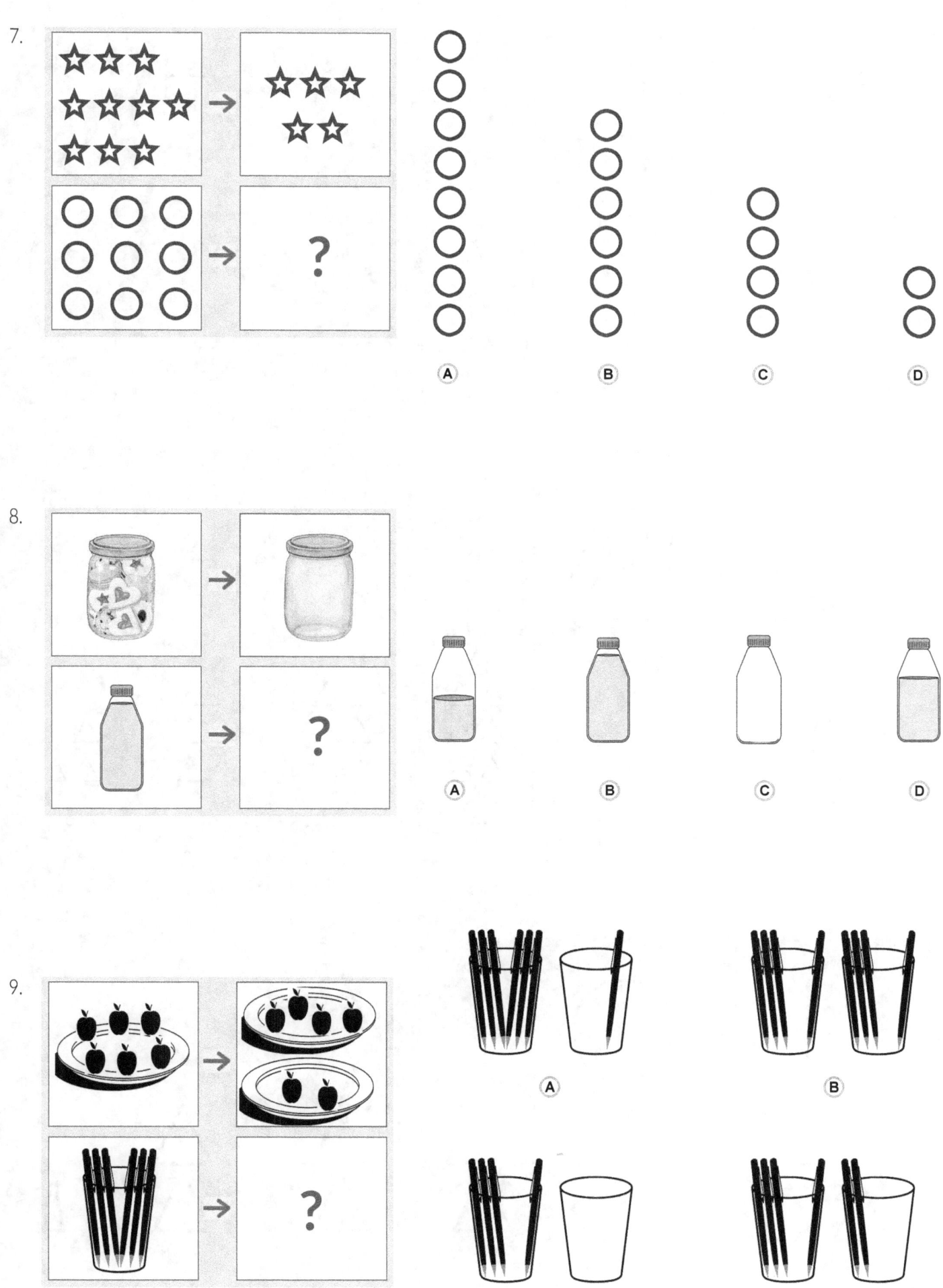

A    B    C    D

8.

A    B    C    D

9.

A    B

C    D

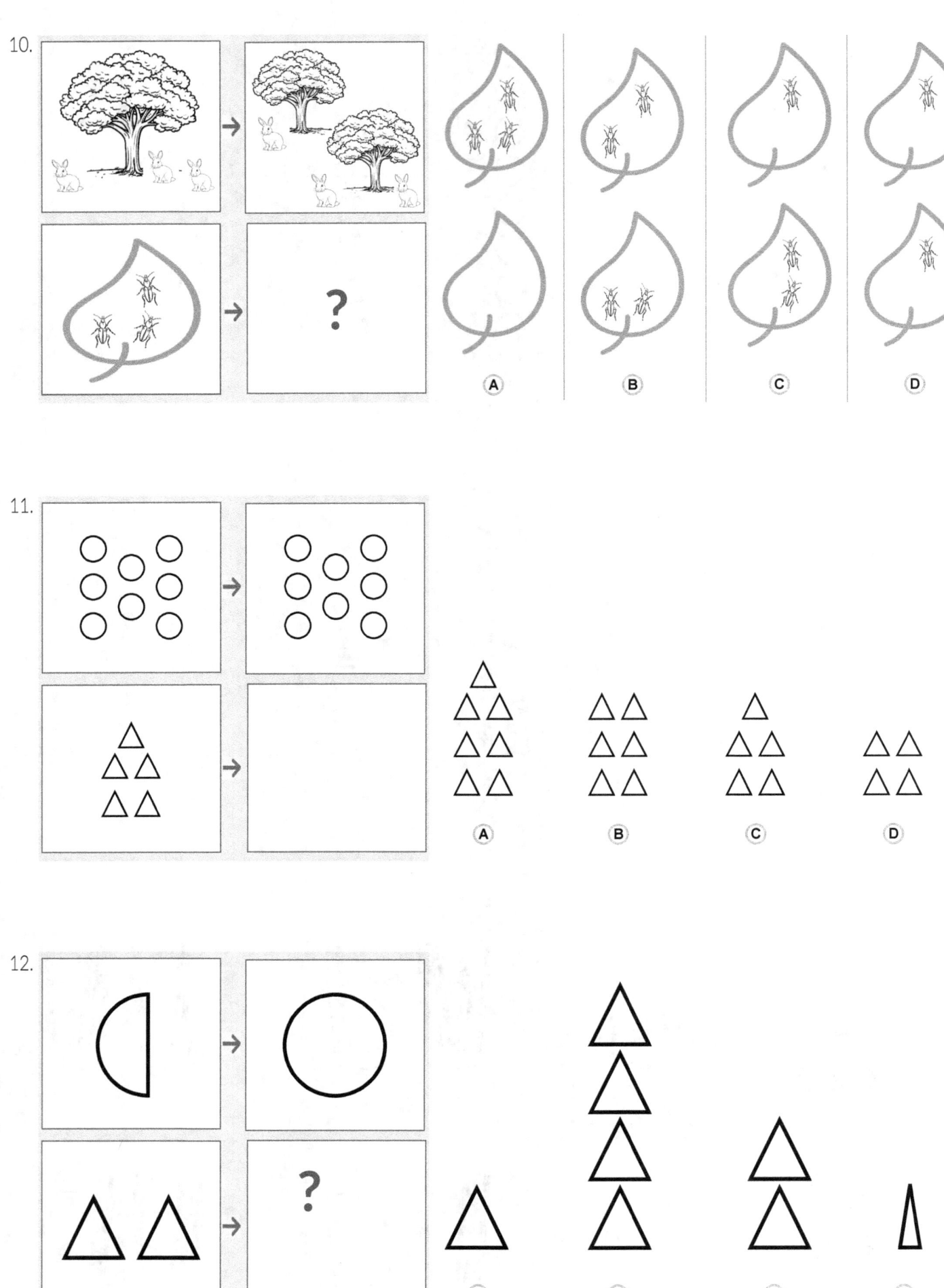

10.

11.

12.

32

13.

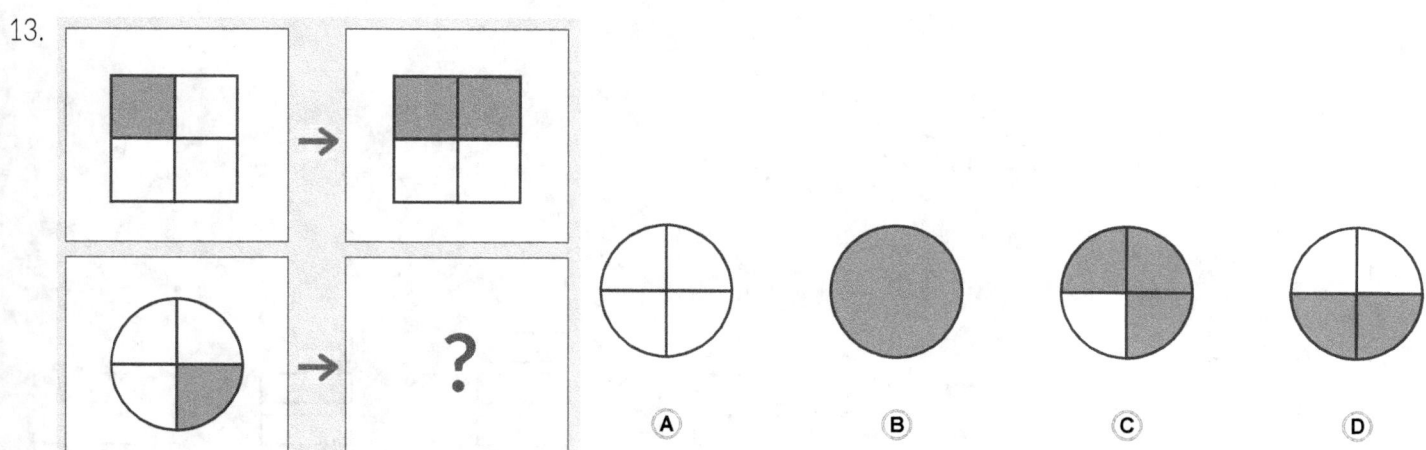

14.

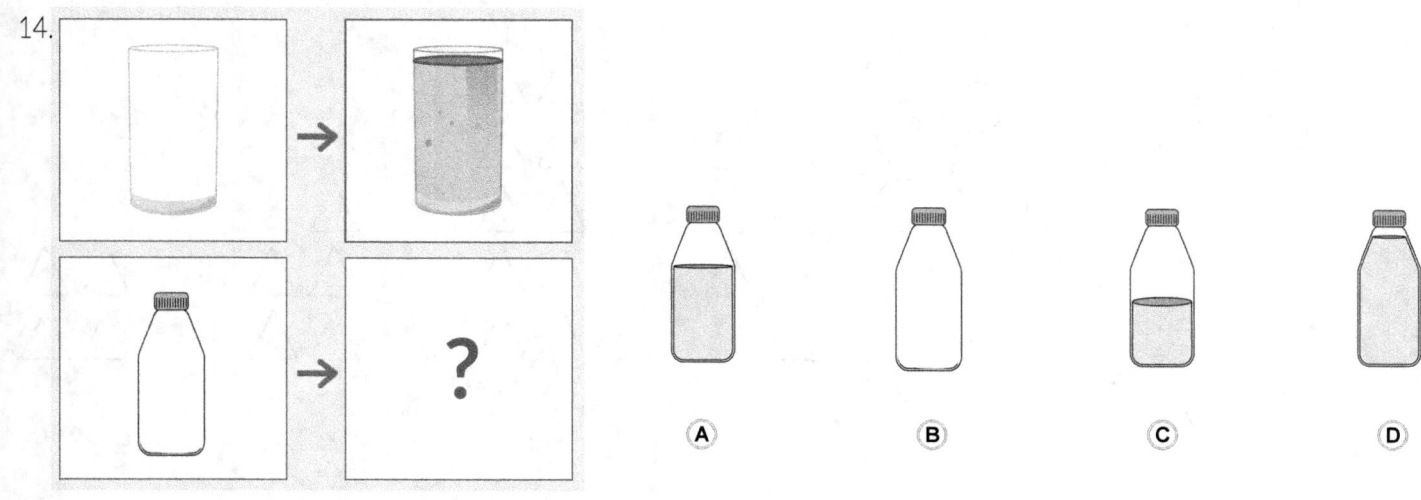

15.

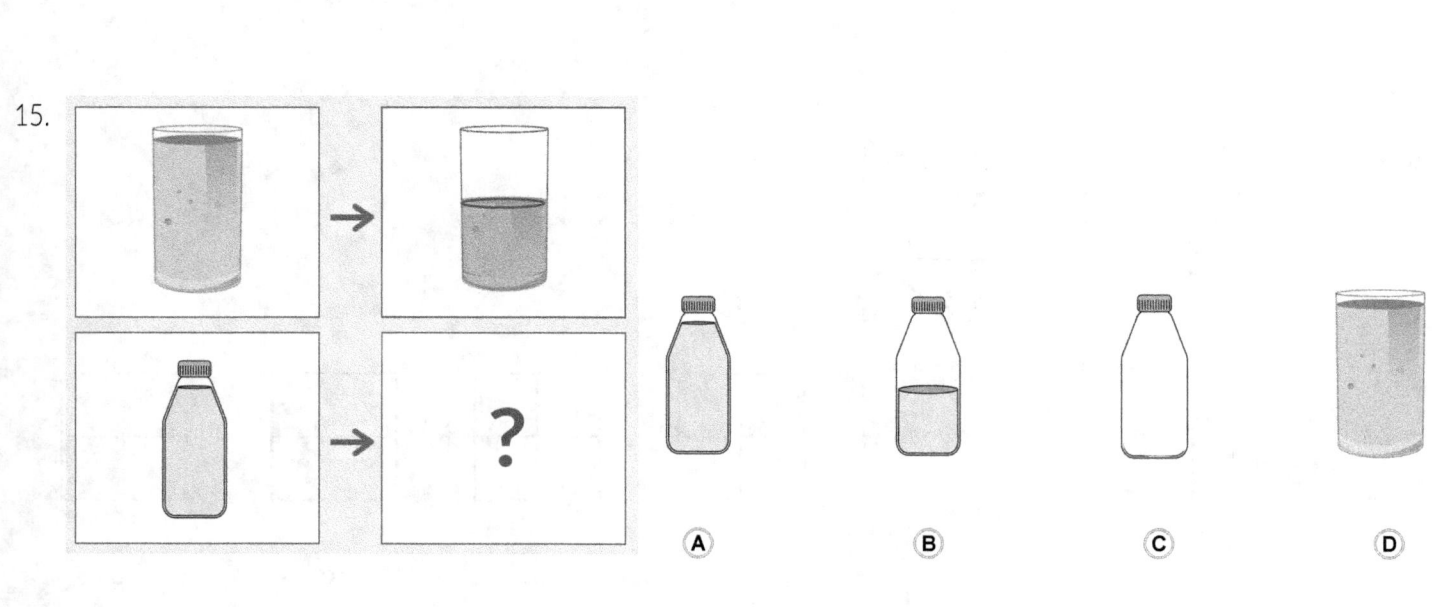

33

16.

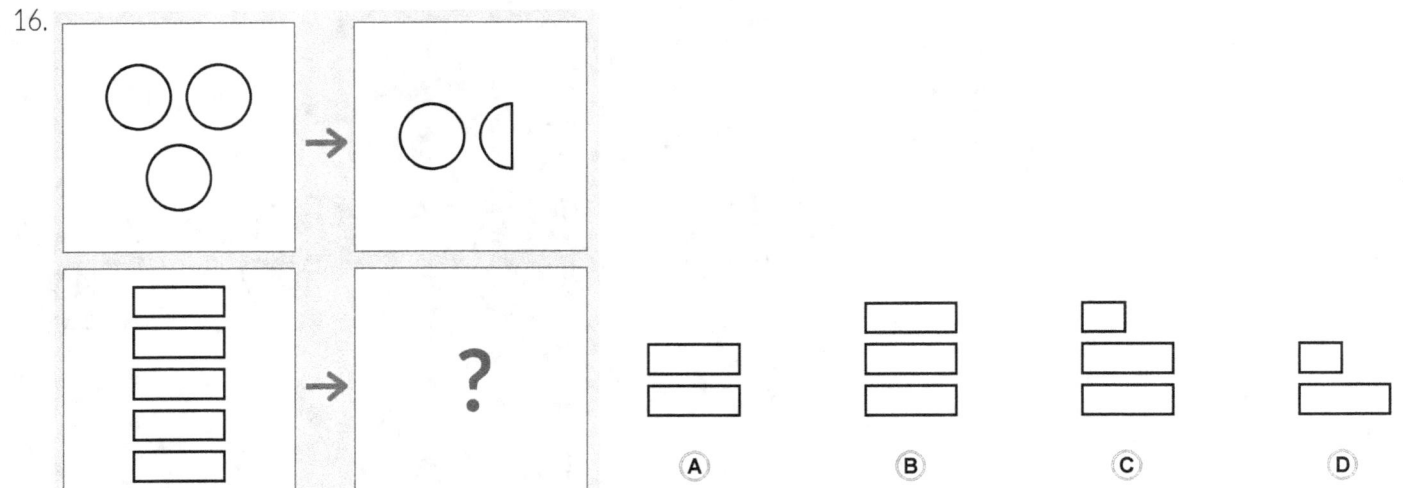

17.

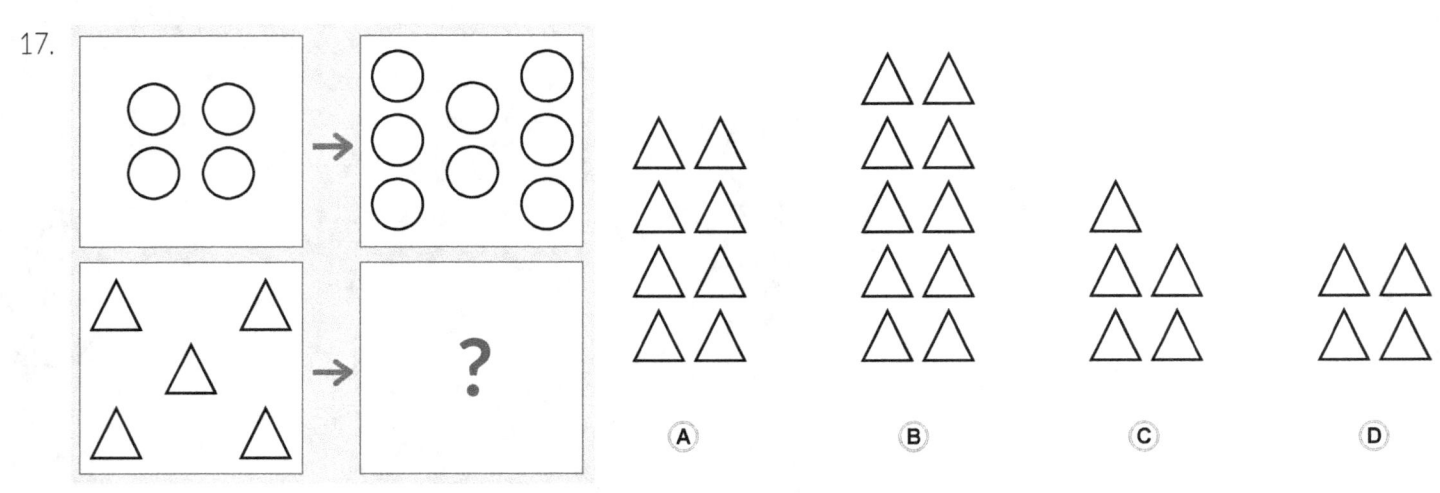

18.

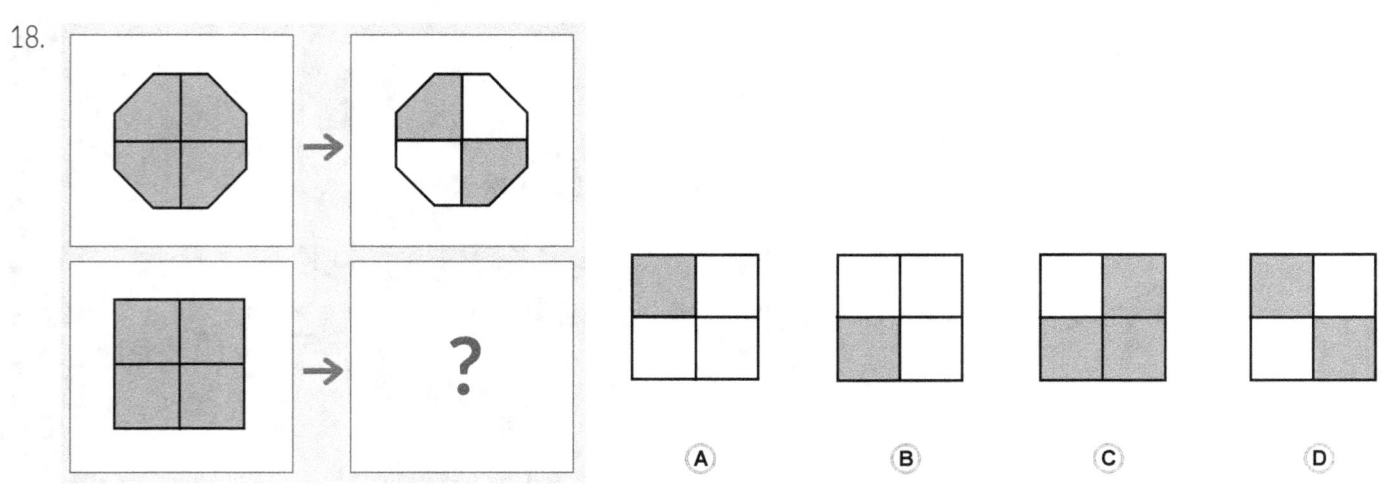

34

# NUMBER PUZZLES  Which train car would make the top and bottom trains carry the same amount?

1.

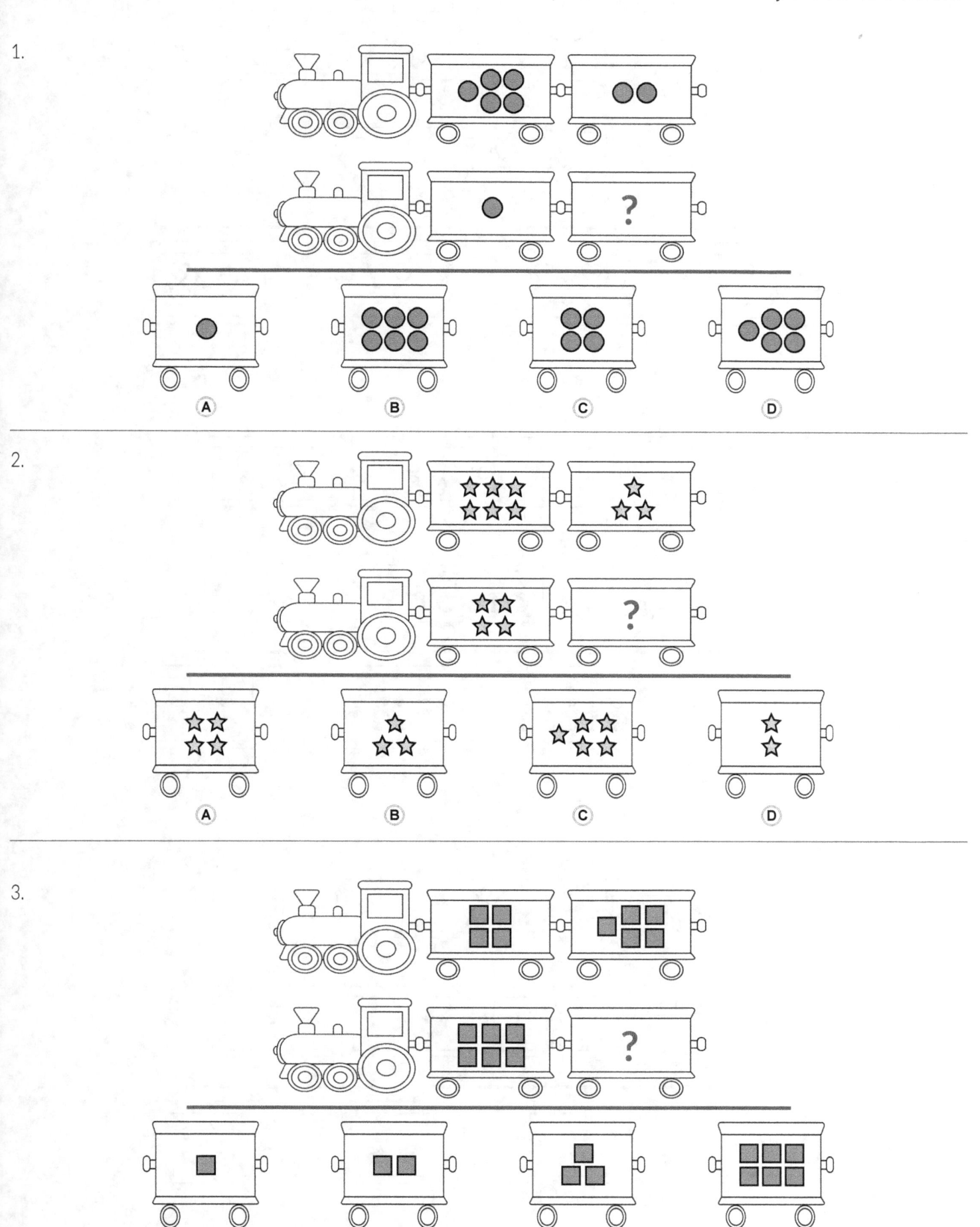

2.

3.

4.

5.

6.

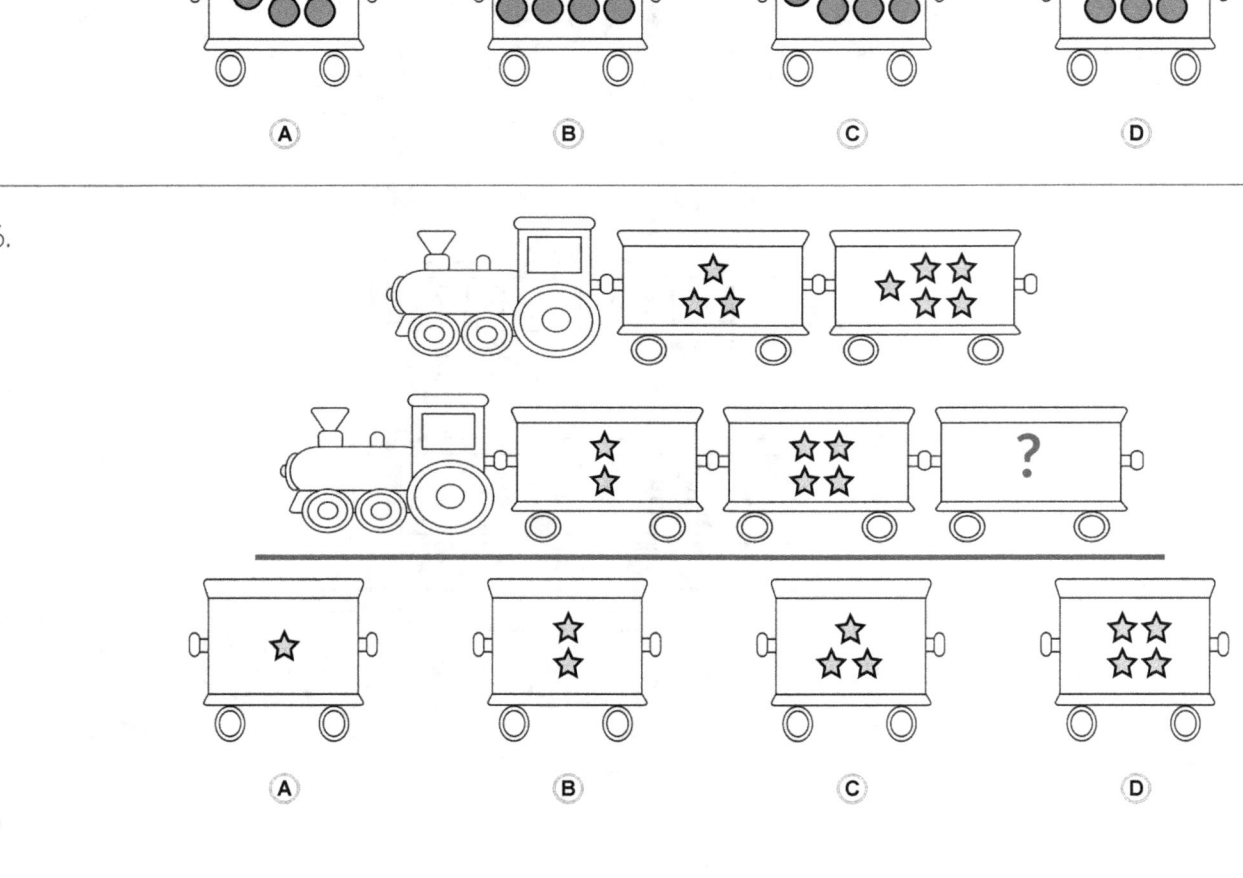

A  B  C  D

7.

A    B    C    D

8.

A    B    C    D

9.

A    B    C    D

37

10.

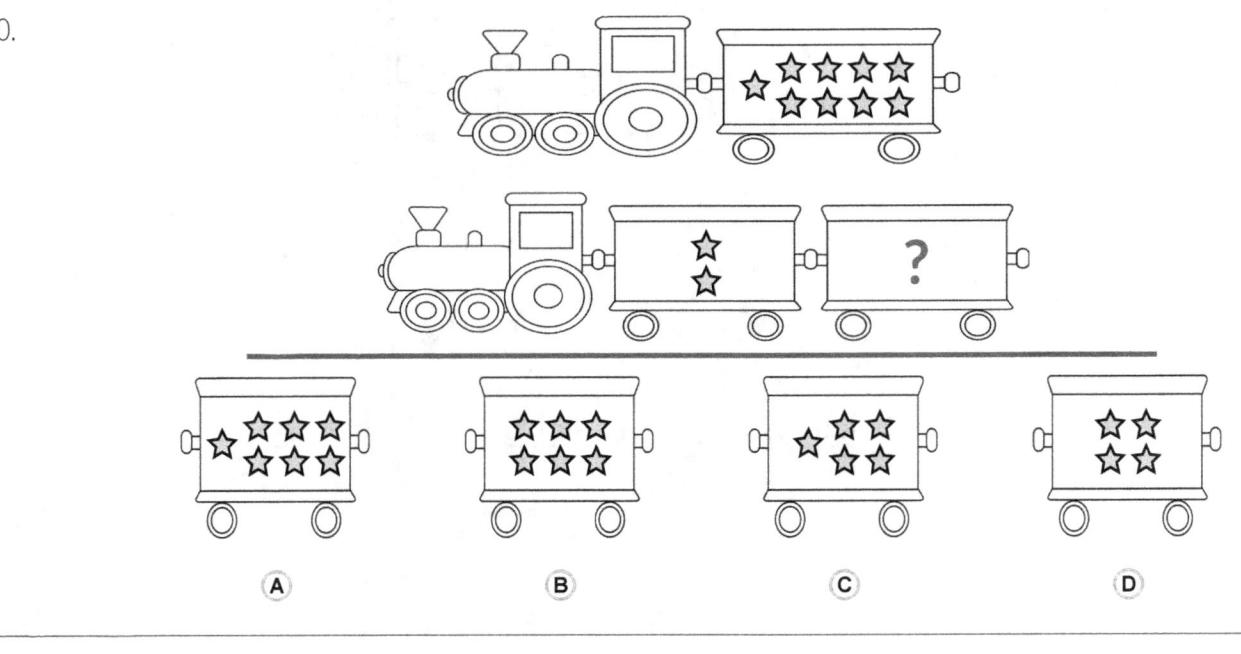

| A | B | C | D |
|---|---|---|---|

11.

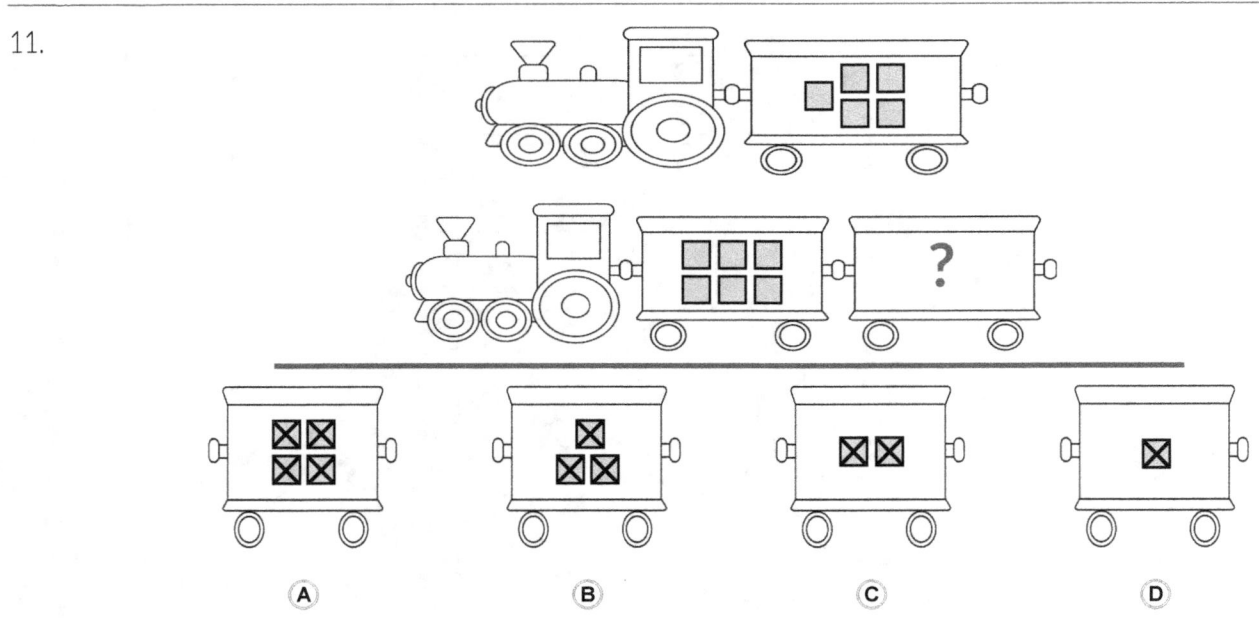

| A | B | C | D |
|---|---|---|---|

12.

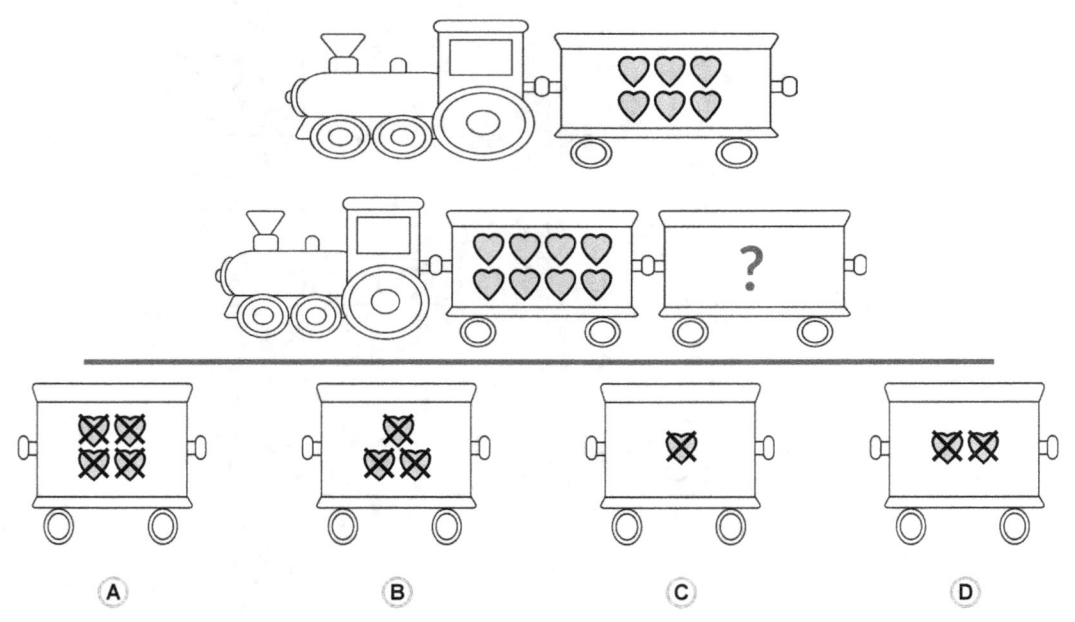

| A | B | C | D |
|---|---|---|---|

# NUMBER PATTERNS

Directions: Which rod goes in the place of the missing rod to finish the pattern?

**1.**

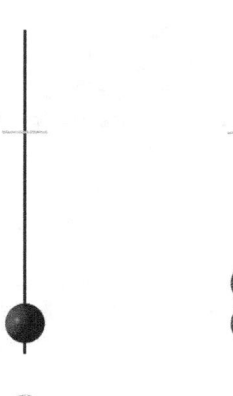 

(A)   (B)   (C)   (D)

**2.**

(A)   (B)   (C)   (D)

**3.**

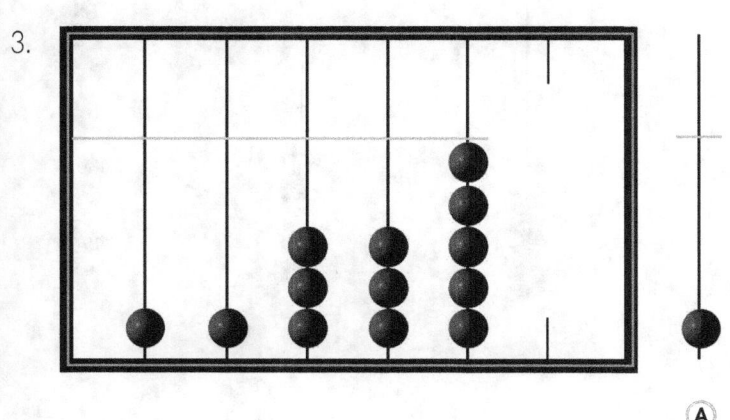   

(A)   (B)   (C)   (D)

4.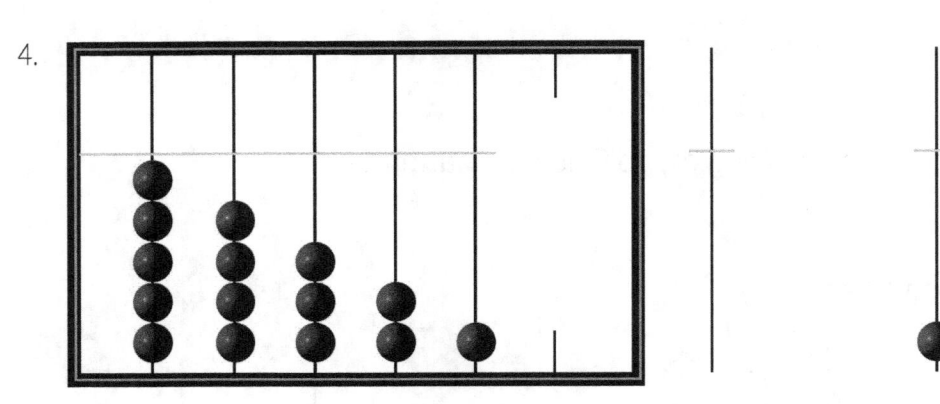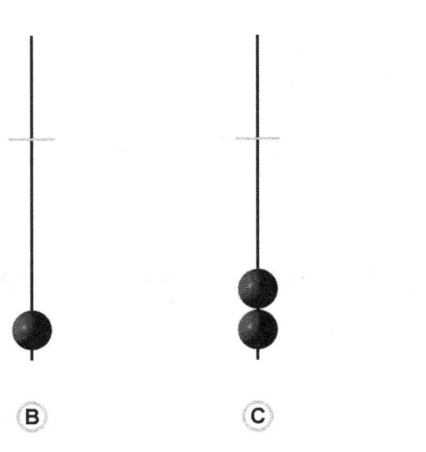

    (A)        (B)        (C)        (D)

5.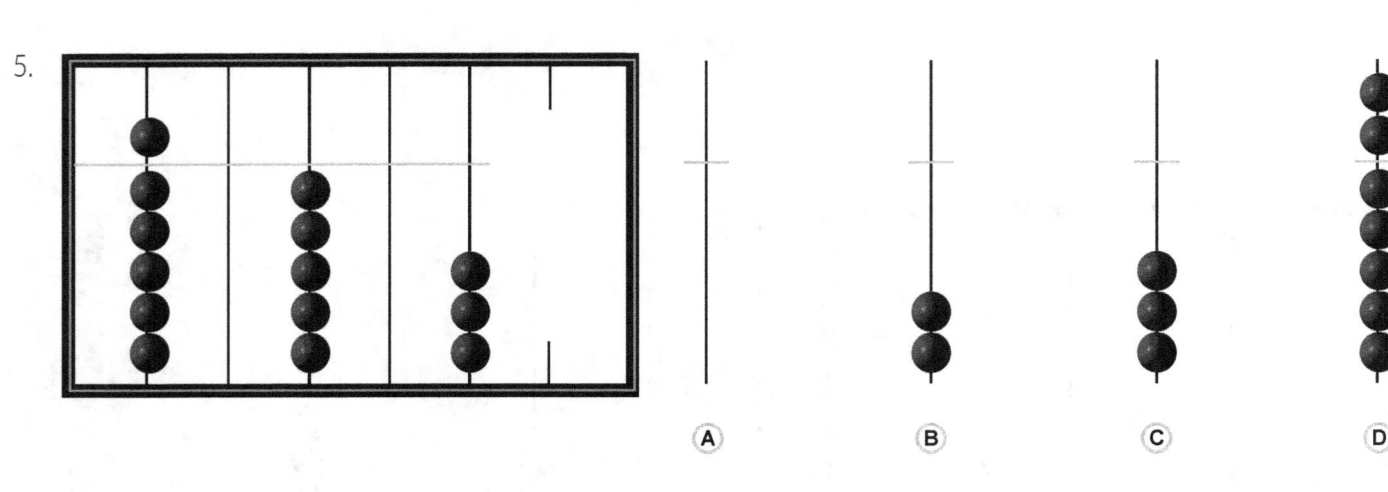

    (A)        (B)        (C)        (D)

6.

    (A)        (B)        (C)        (D)

7.

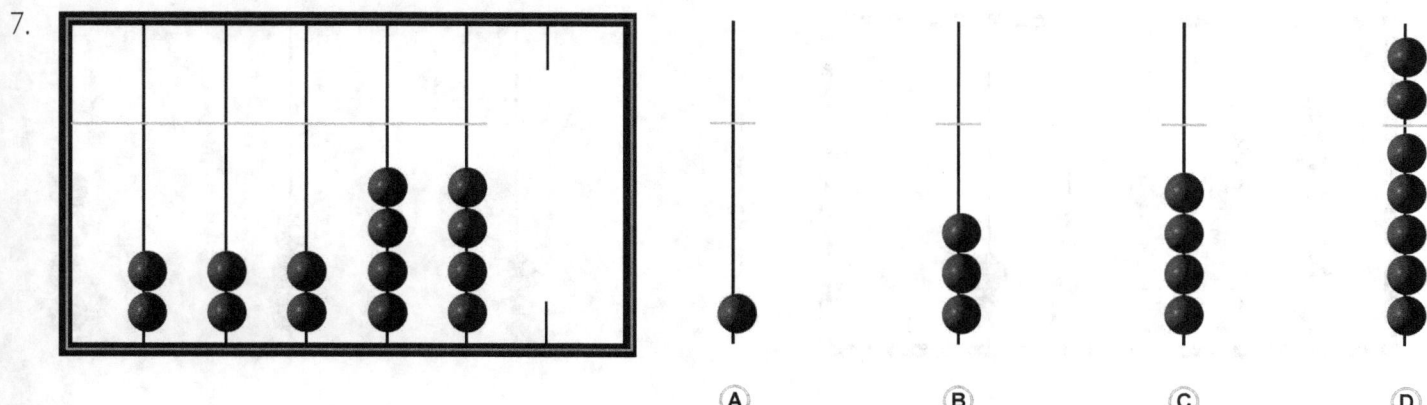

(A)     (B)     (C)     (D)

8.

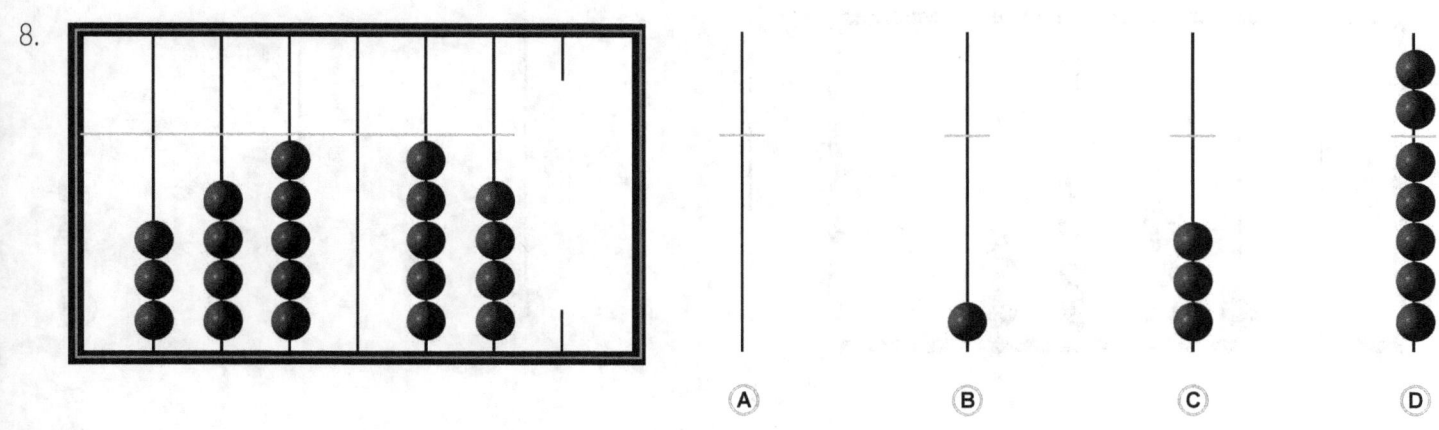

(A)     (B)     (C)     (D)

9.

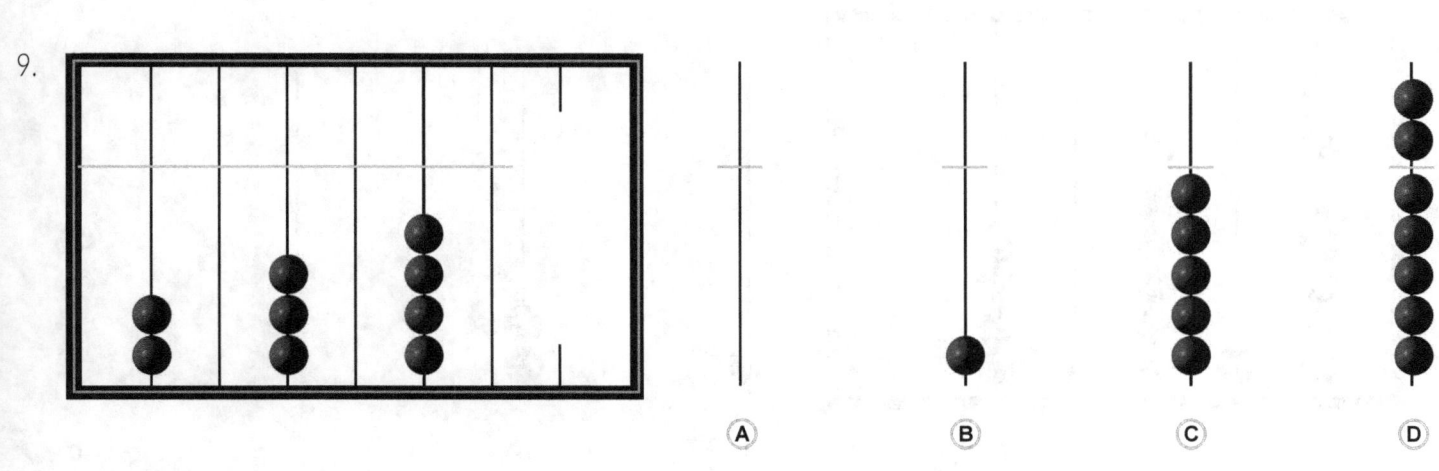

(A)     (B)     (C)     (D)

41

10.

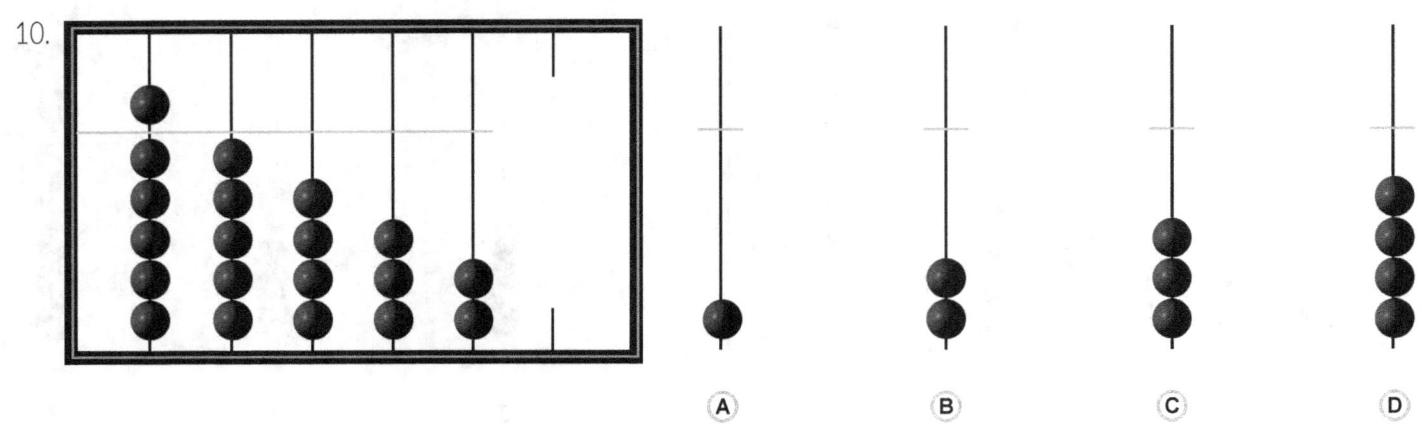

A     B     C     D

11.

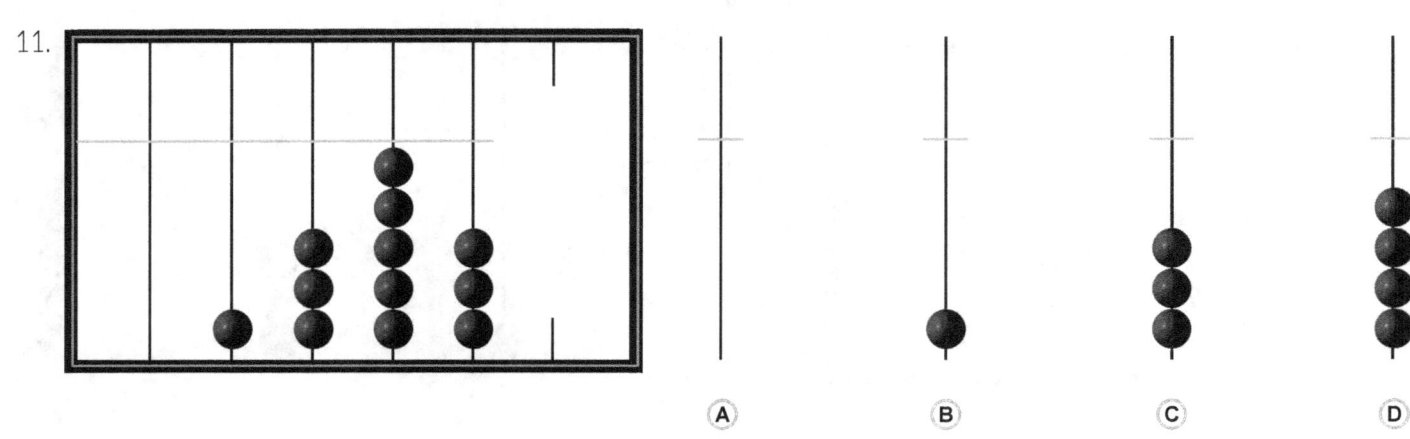

A     B     C     D

12.

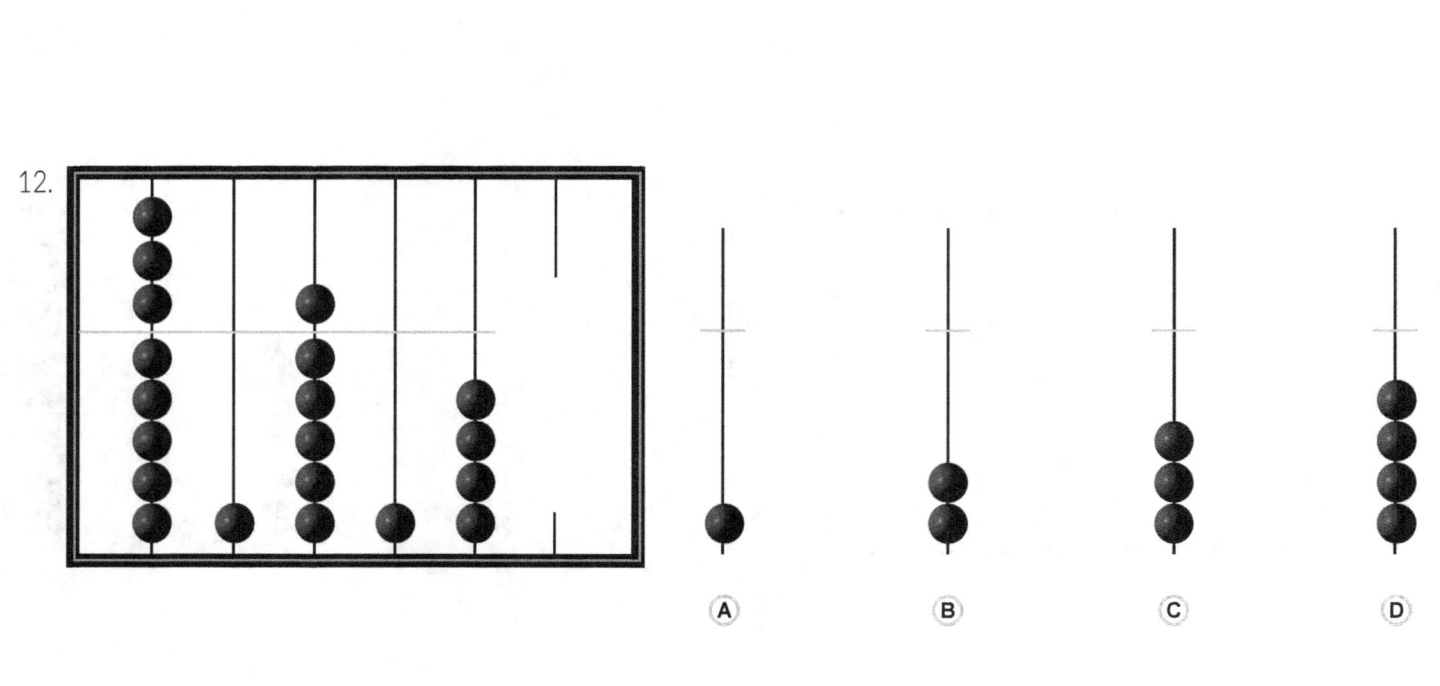

A     B     C     D

13.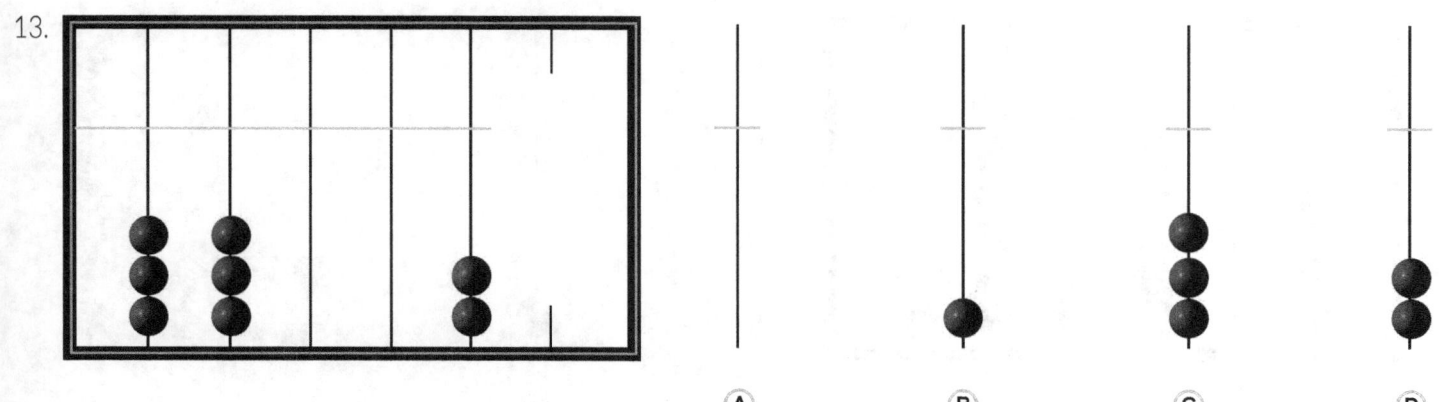

A     B     C     D

14.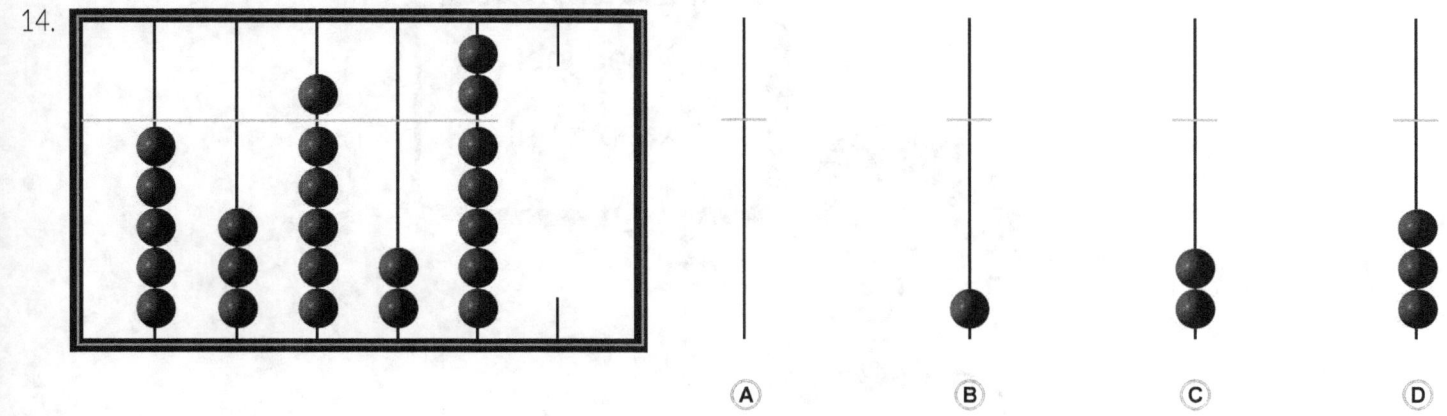

A     B     C     D

15.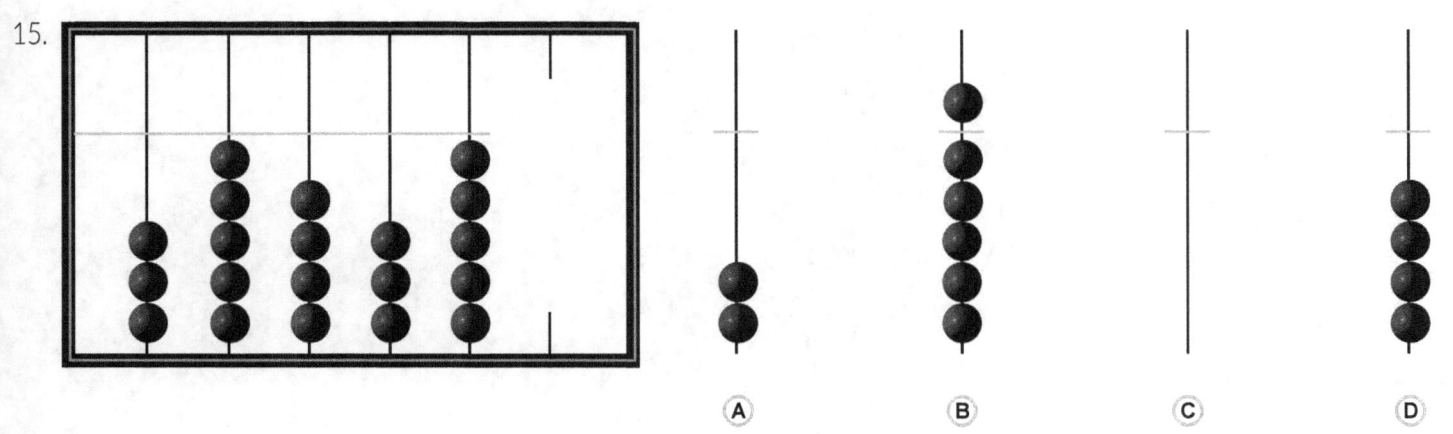

A     B     C     D

16.

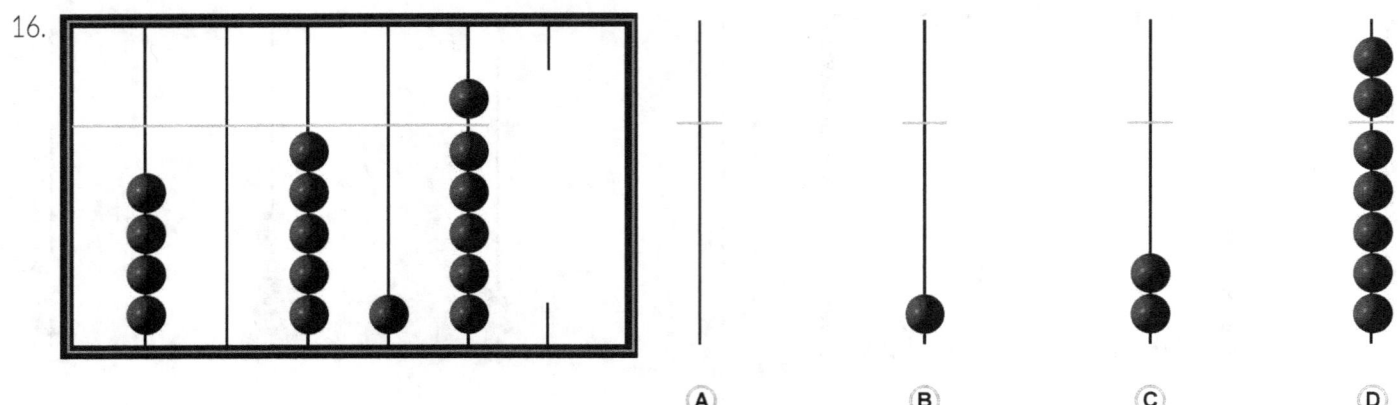

(A)   (B)   (C)   (D)

Good job!

Keep it up!

Caleb

- End of Practice Test 2. -

COGAT® Practice Test 3

Directions: The pictures in the top boxes go together in some way. One of the bottom boxes is empty.
Which answer choice goes with the picture in the bottom box in the same way the top pictures do?

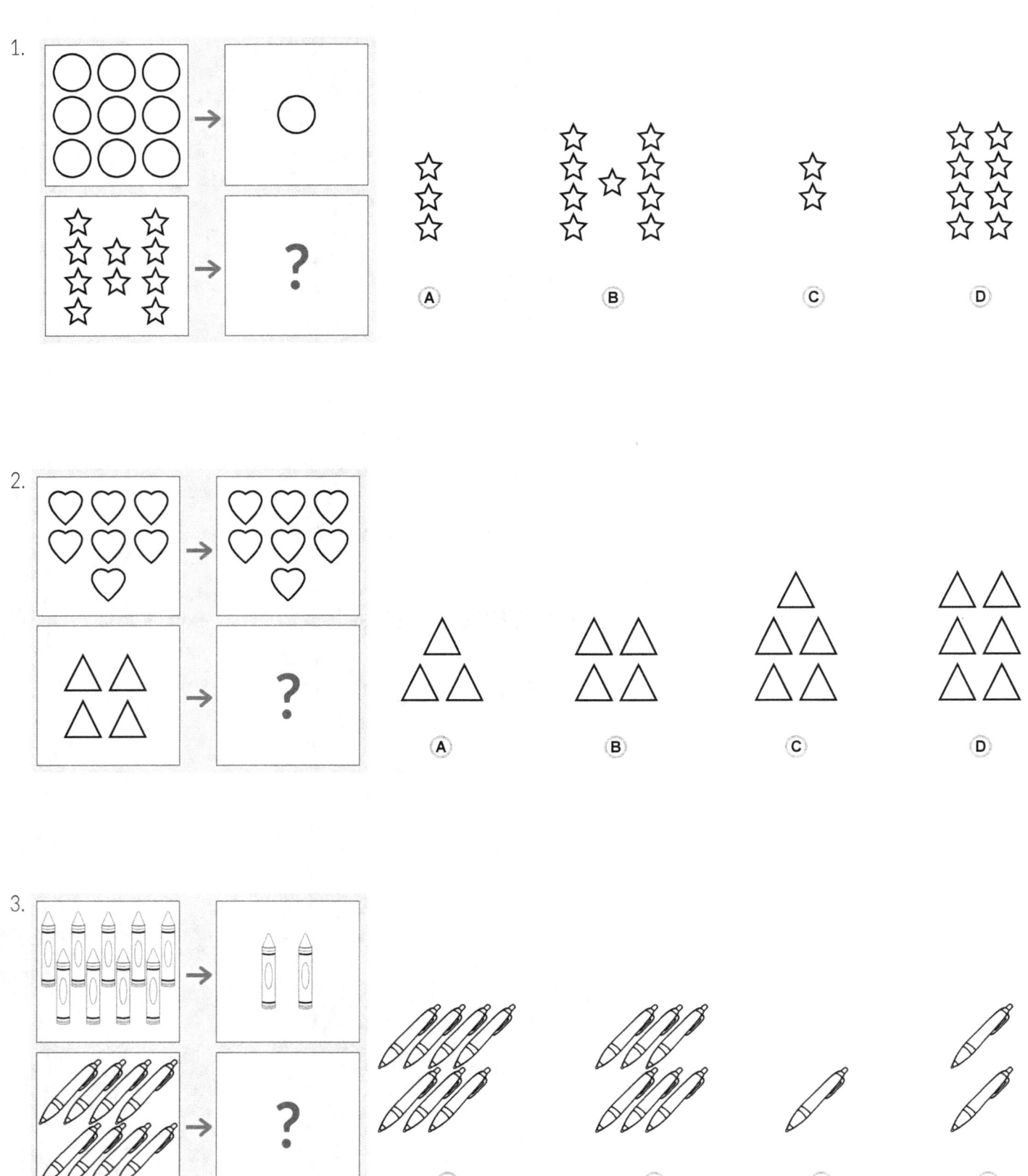

4.

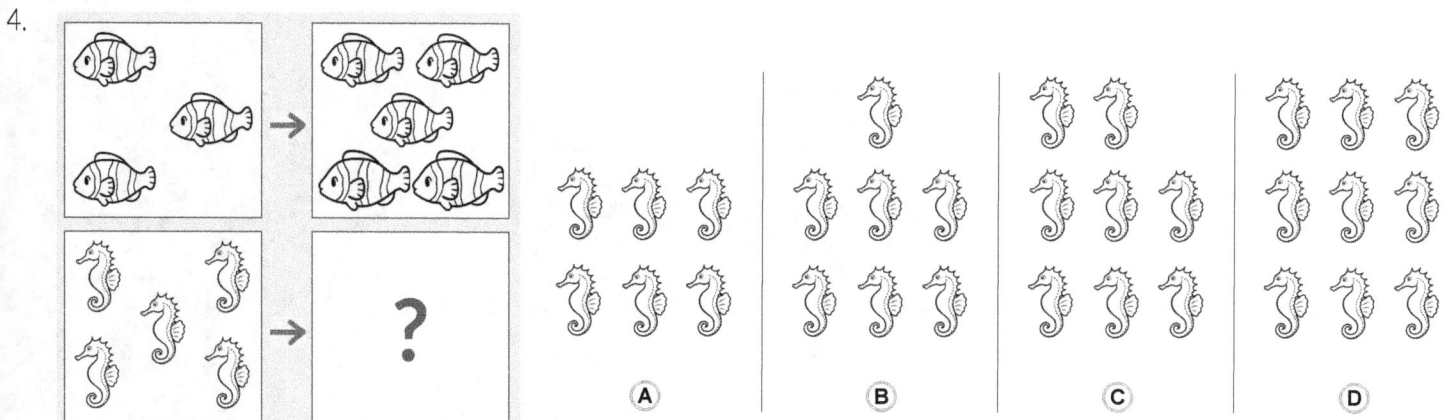

5.

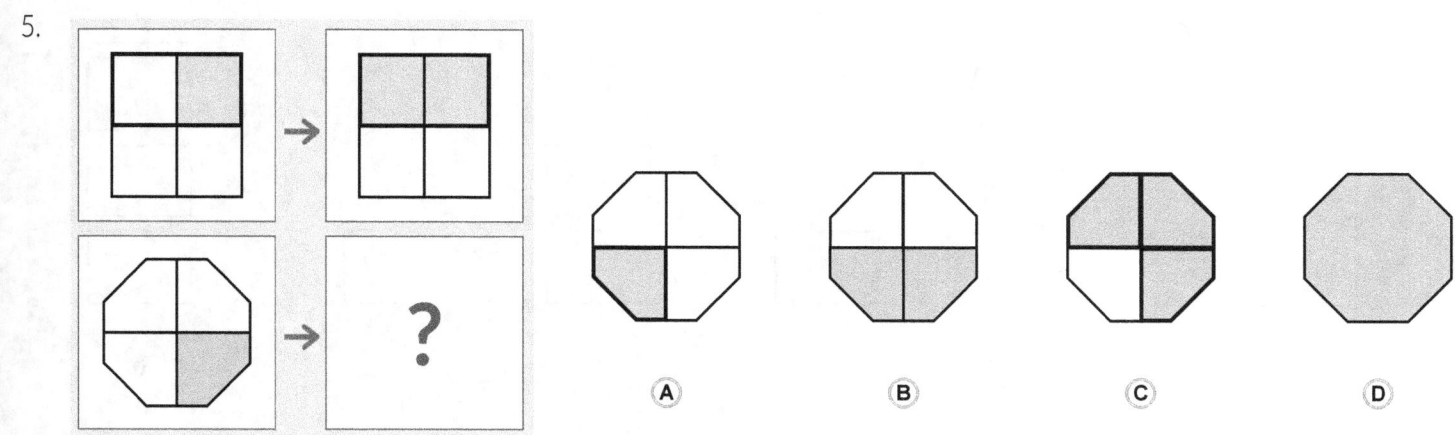

6.

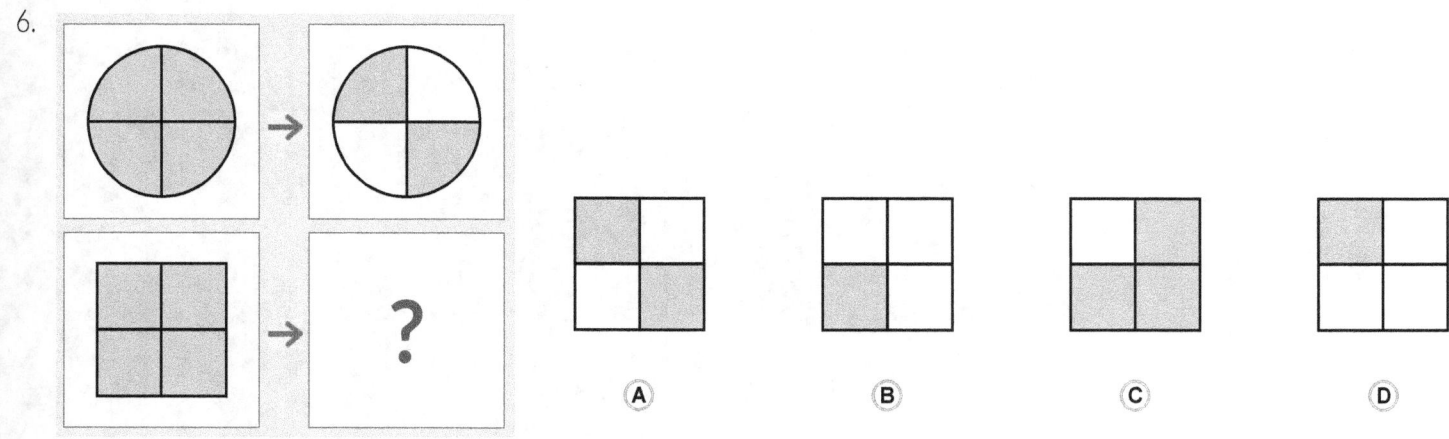

47

7.

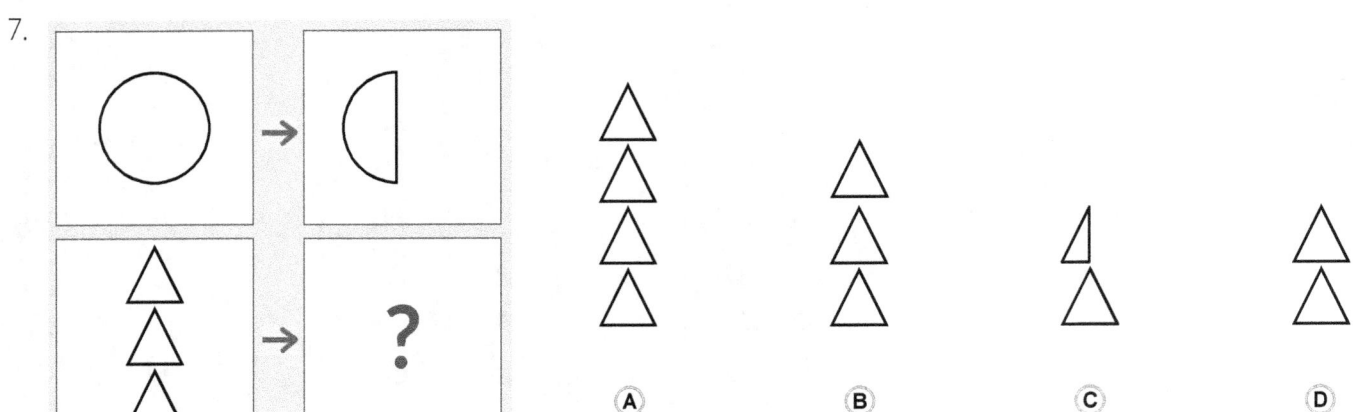

Ⓐ  Ⓑ  Ⓒ  Ⓓ

8.

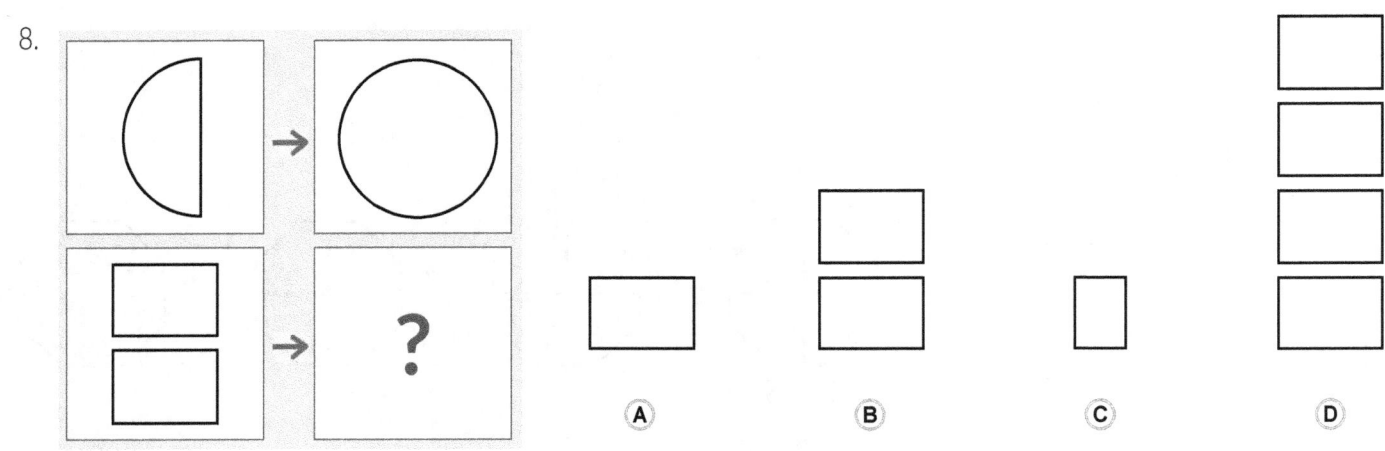

Ⓐ  Ⓑ  Ⓒ  Ⓓ

9.

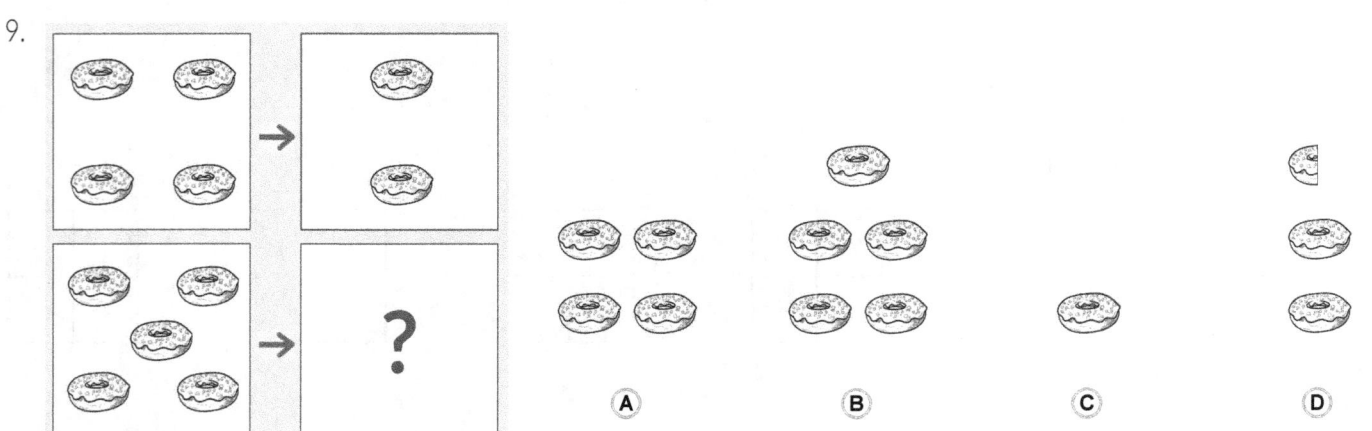

Ⓐ  Ⓑ  Ⓒ  Ⓓ

10.

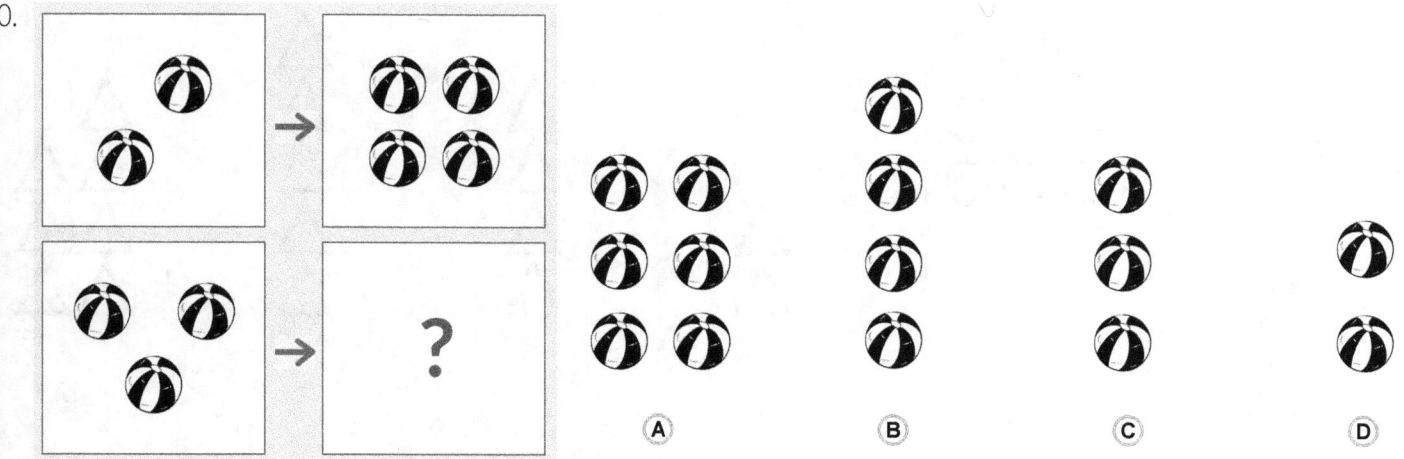

A   B   C   D

11.

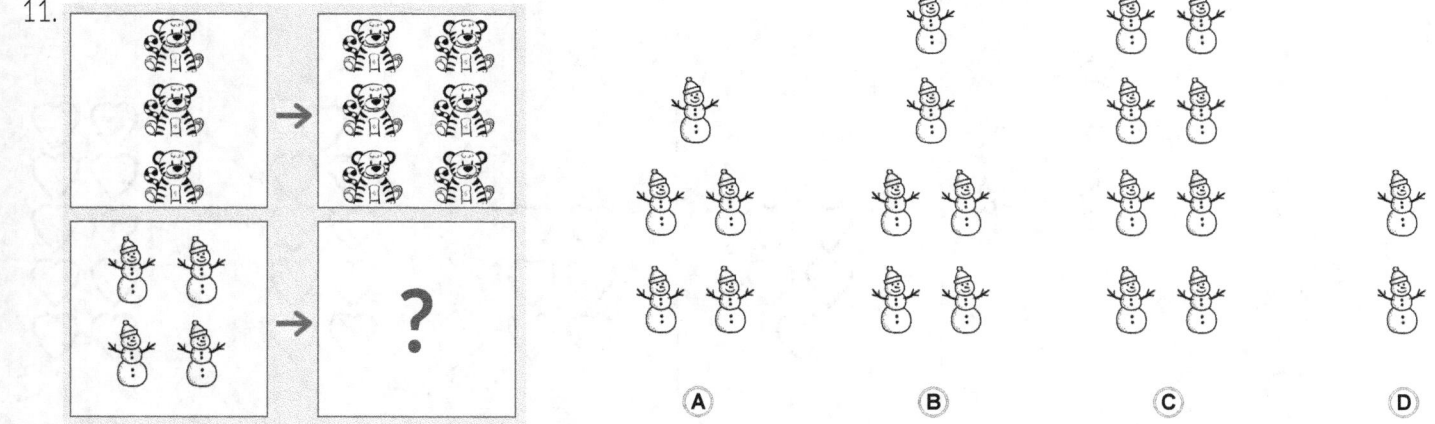

A   B   C   D

12.

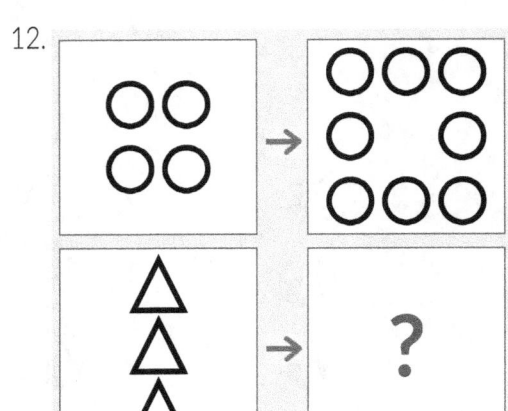

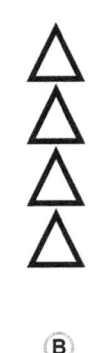

Ⓐ      Ⓑ      Ⓒ      Ⓓ

13.

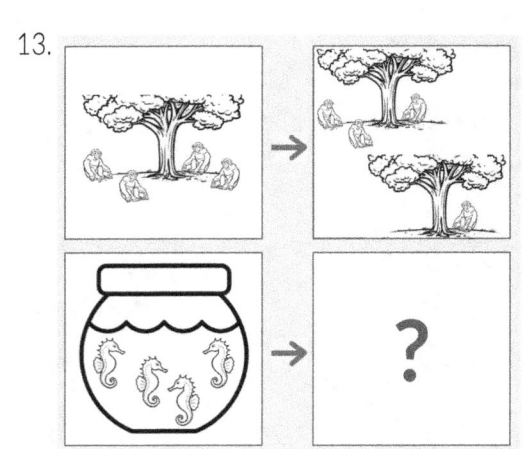

Ⓐ      Ⓑ      Ⓒ      Ⓓ

14.

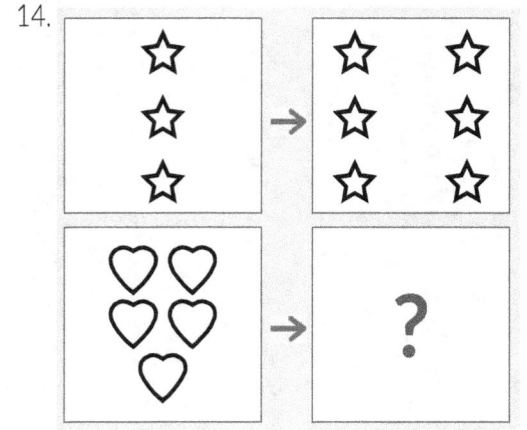

Ⓐ      Ⓑ      Ⓒ      Ⓓ

# NUMBER PUZZLES   Which train car would make the top and bottom trains carry the same amount?

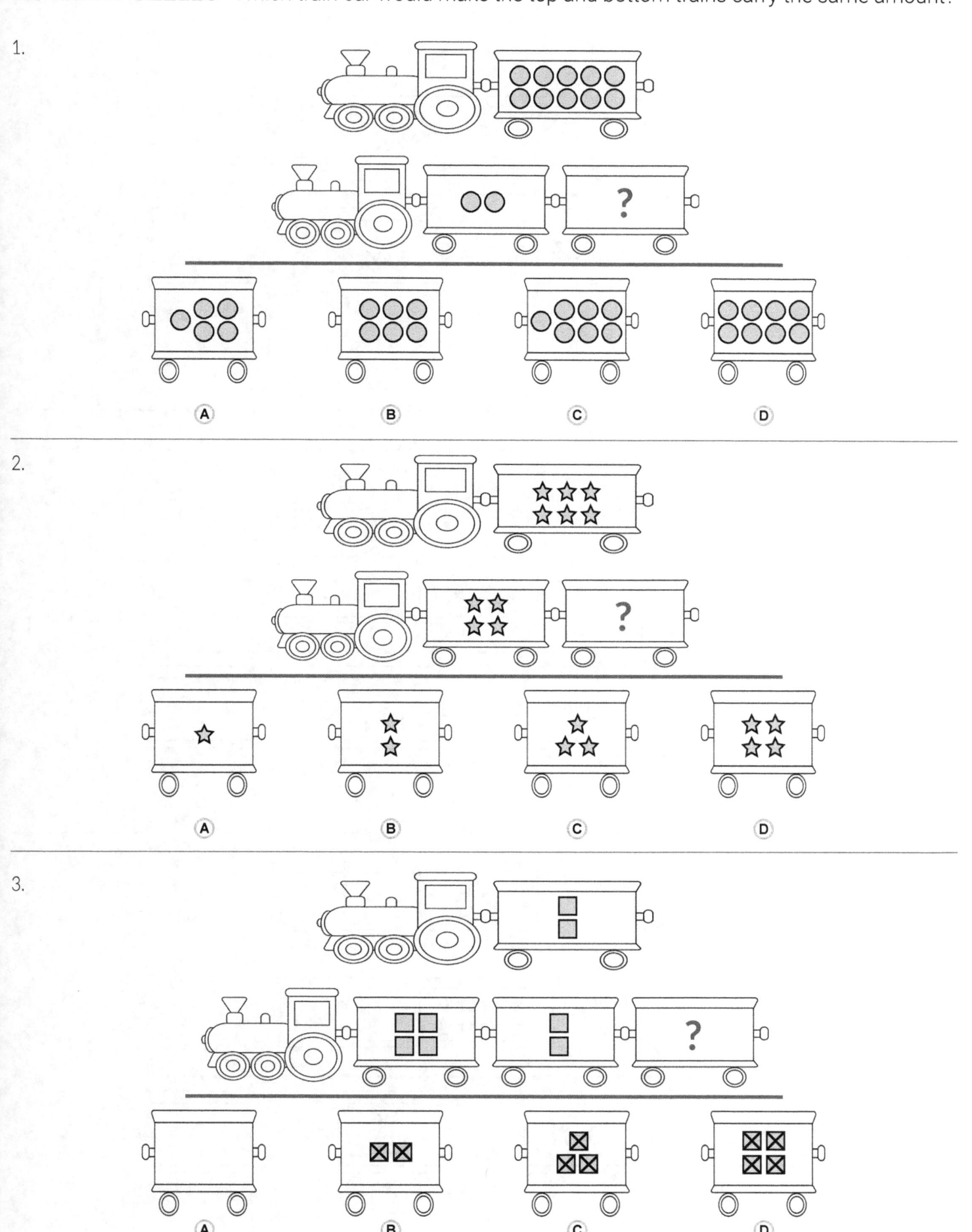

1.

A   B   C   D

2.

A   B   C   D

3.

A   B   C   D

**4.**

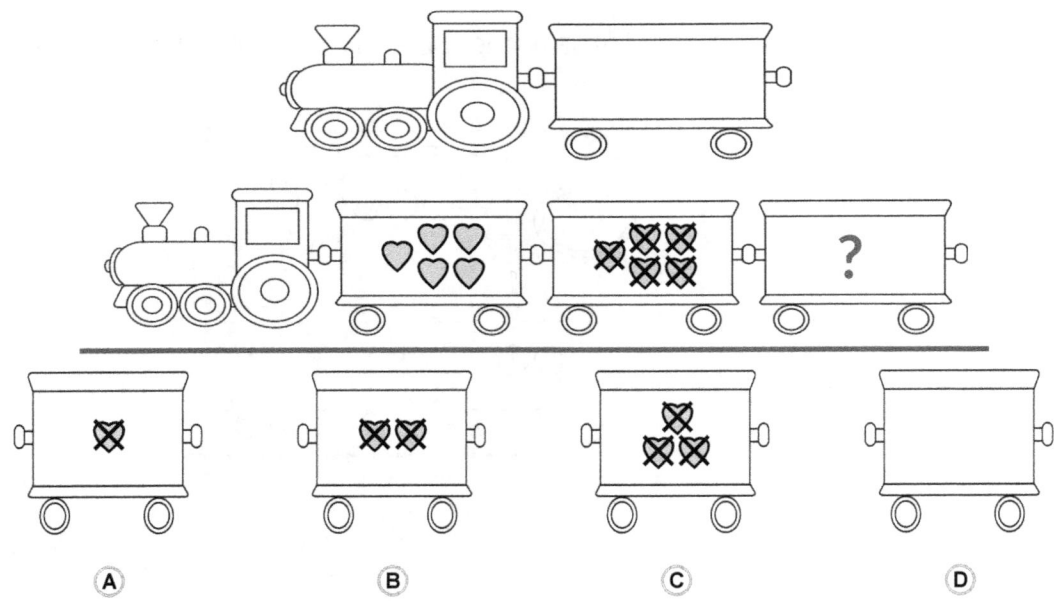

**5.**

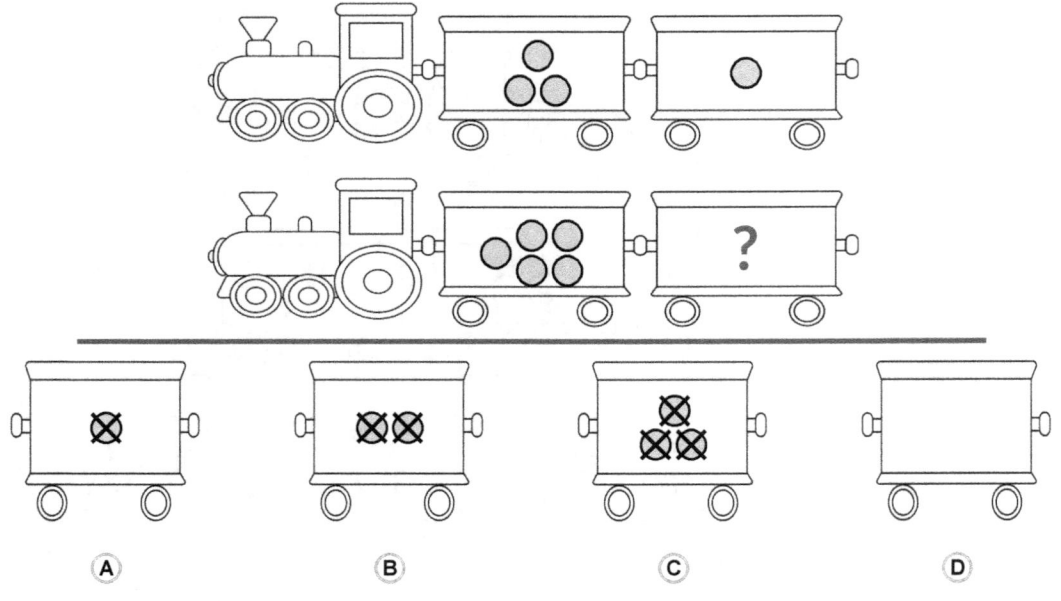

**6.**

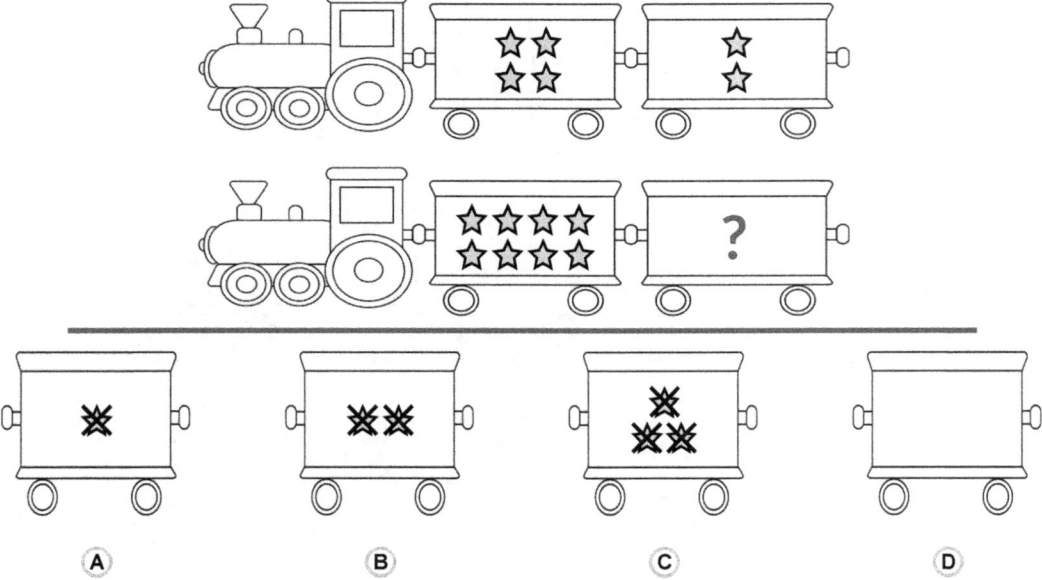

52

7.

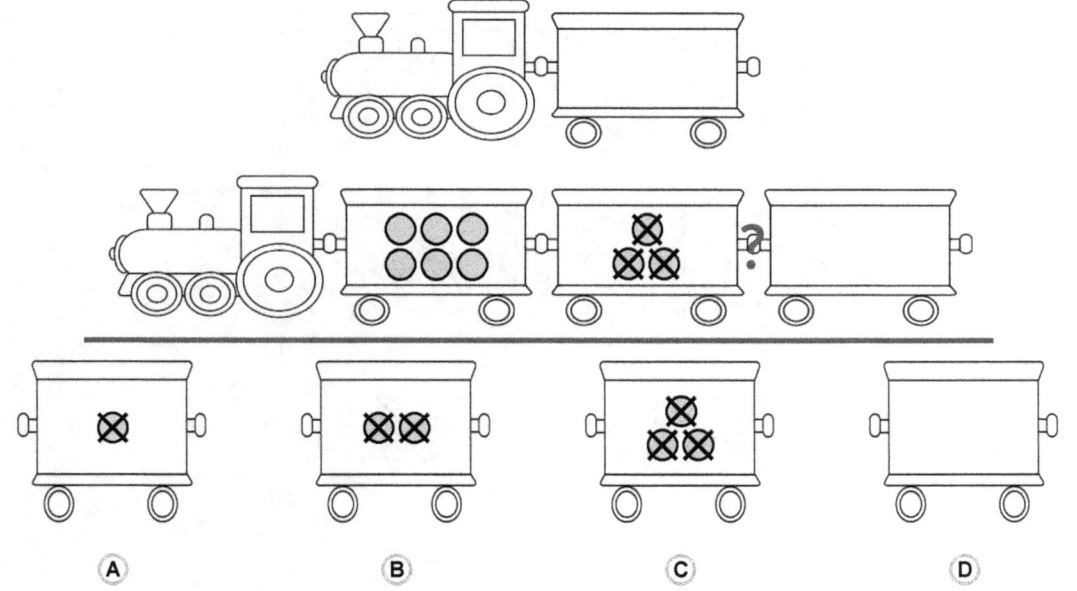

A B C D

8.

A B C D

9.

A B C D

53

**10.**

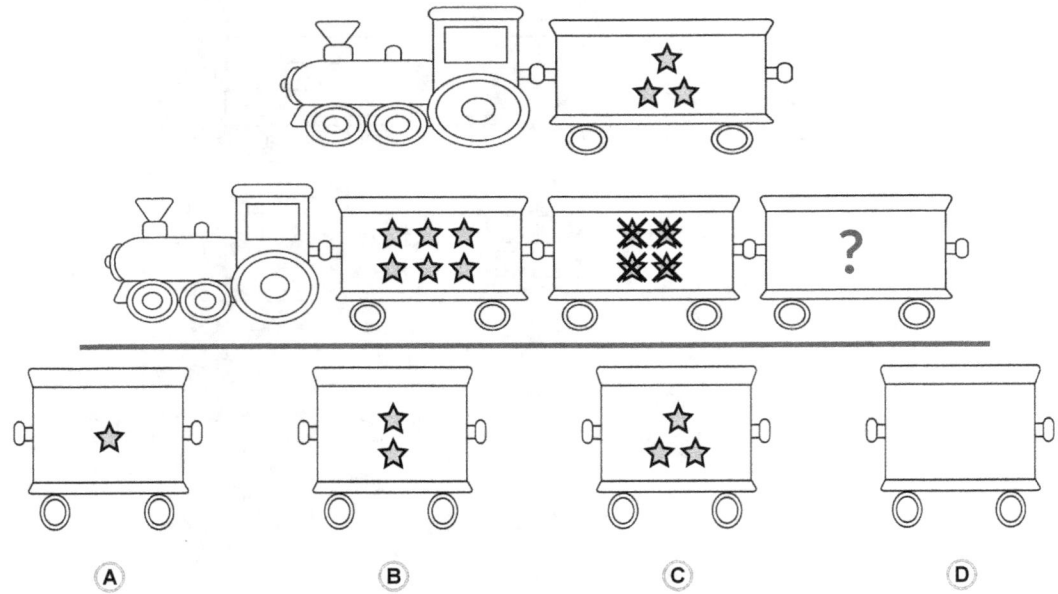

| A | B | C | D |
|---|---|---|---|

**11.**

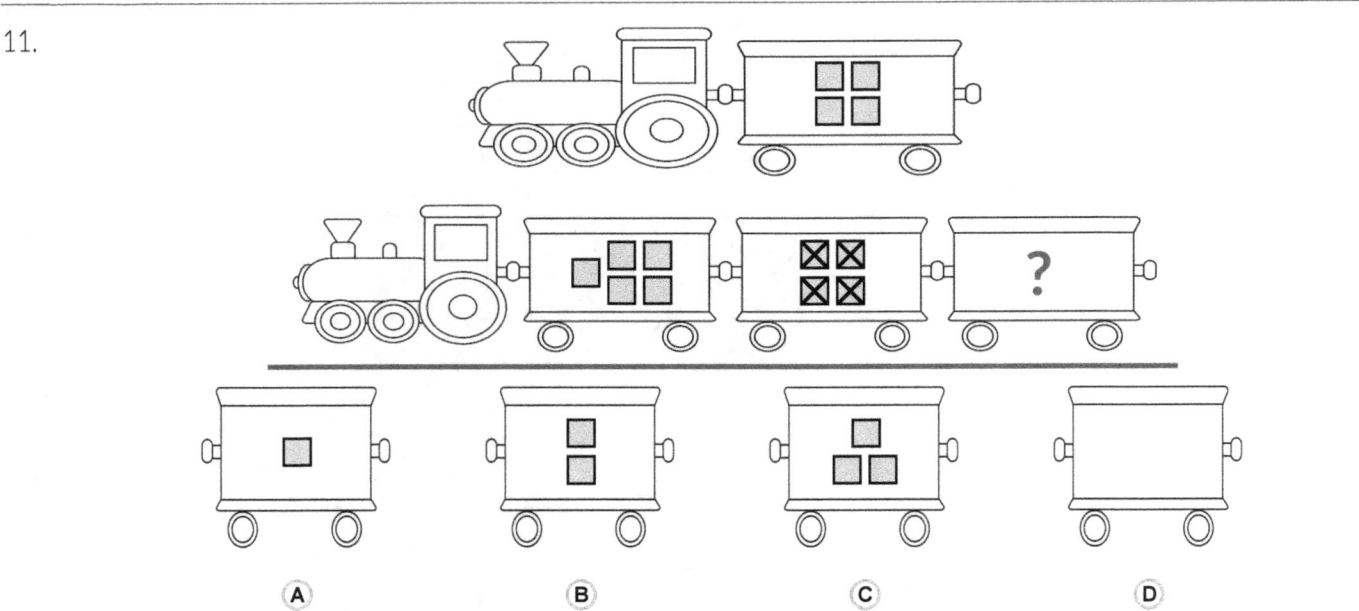

| A | B | C | D |
|---|---|---|---|

**12.**

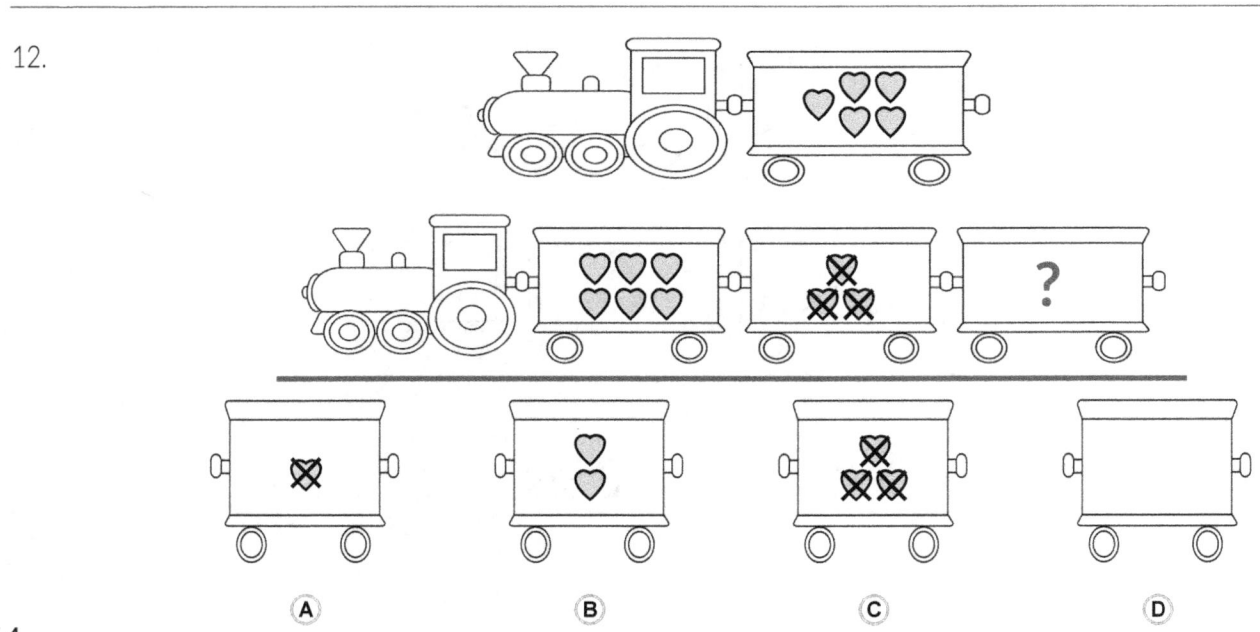

| A | B | C | D |
|---|---|---|---|

# NUMBER PATTERNS

Directions: Which rod goes in the place of the missing rod to finish the pattern?

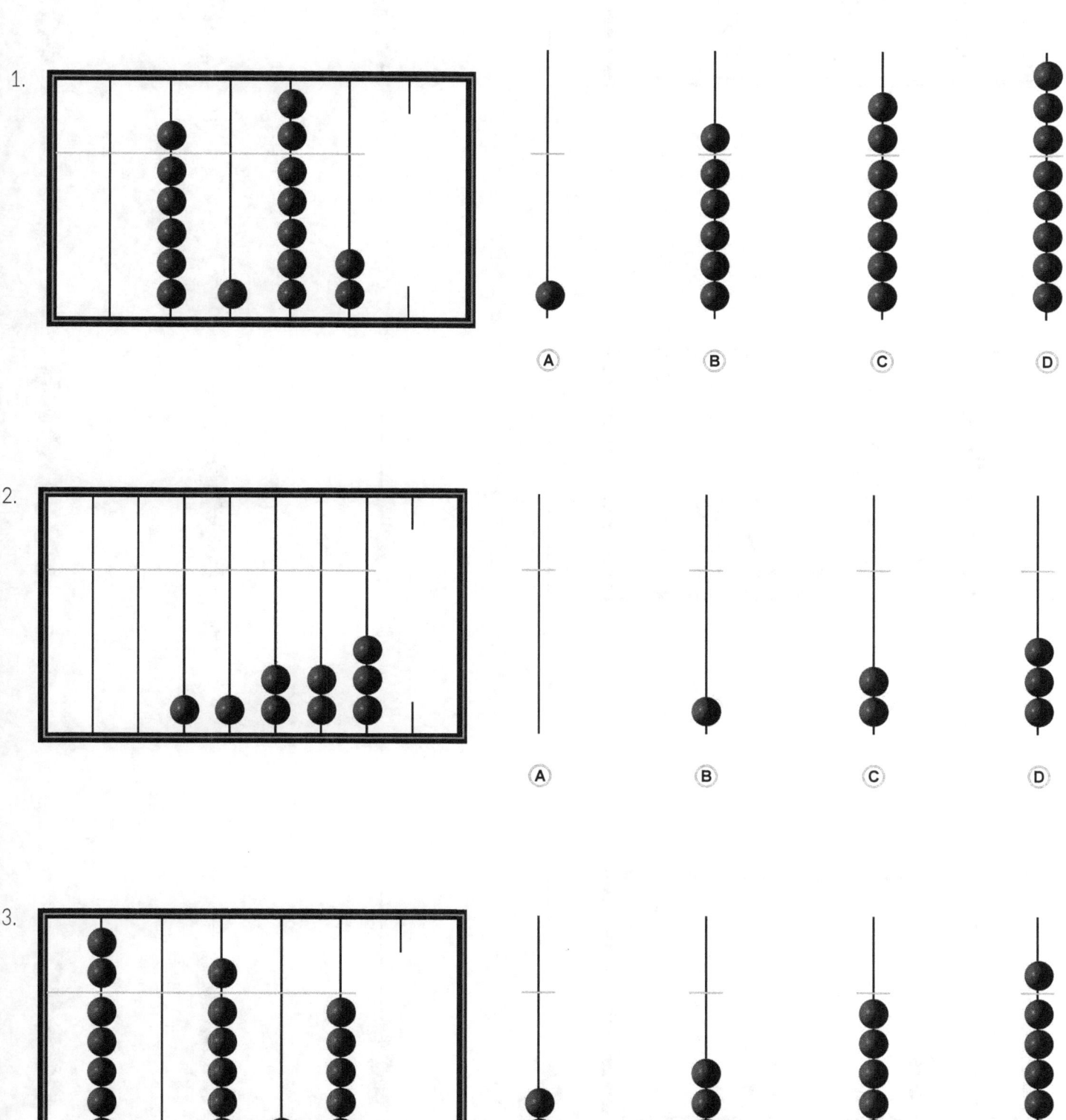

4.

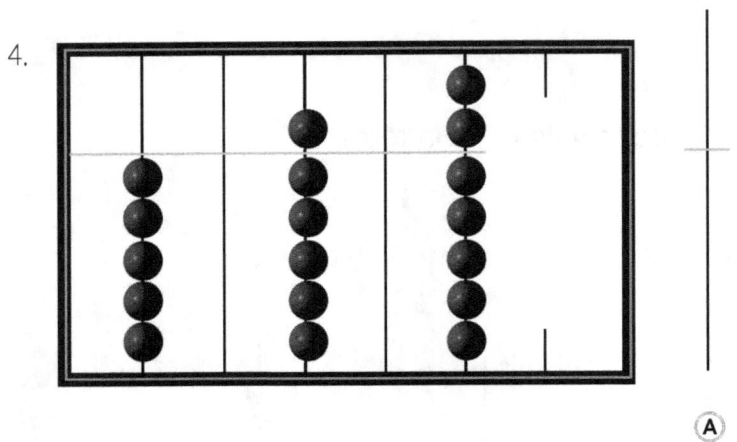 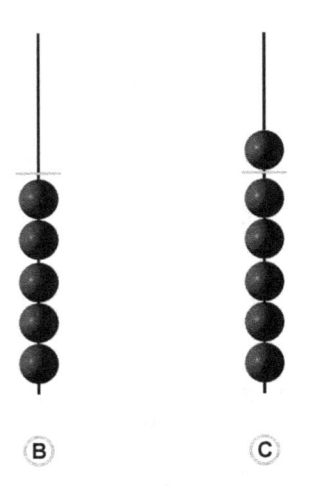 

A   B   C   D

5.

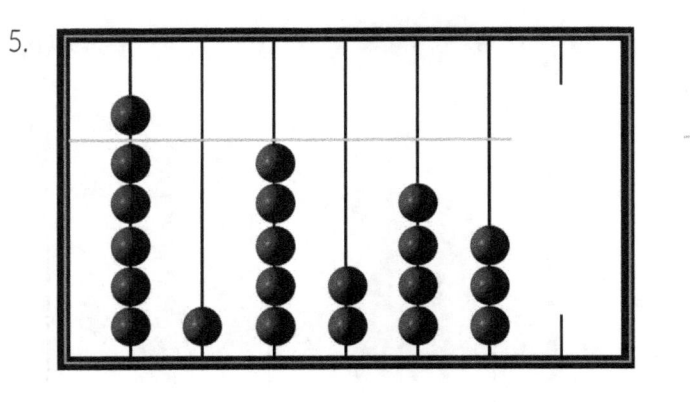 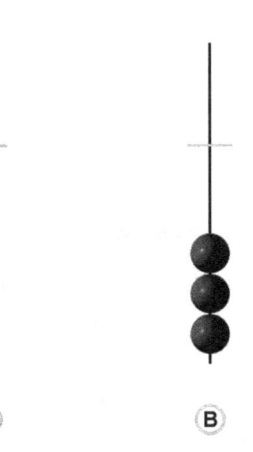 

A   B   C   D

6.

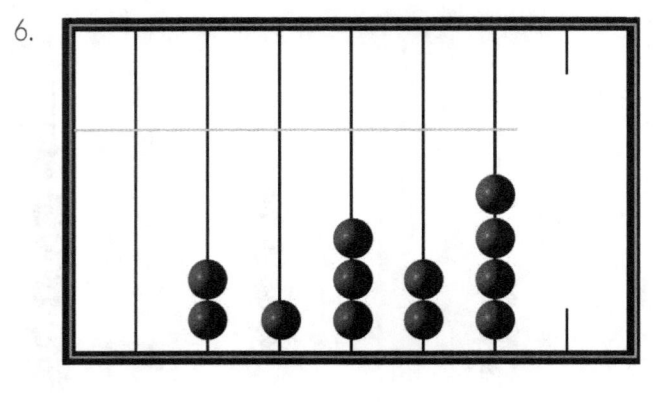 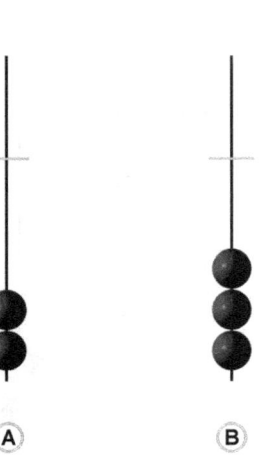  

A   B   C   D

**7.**

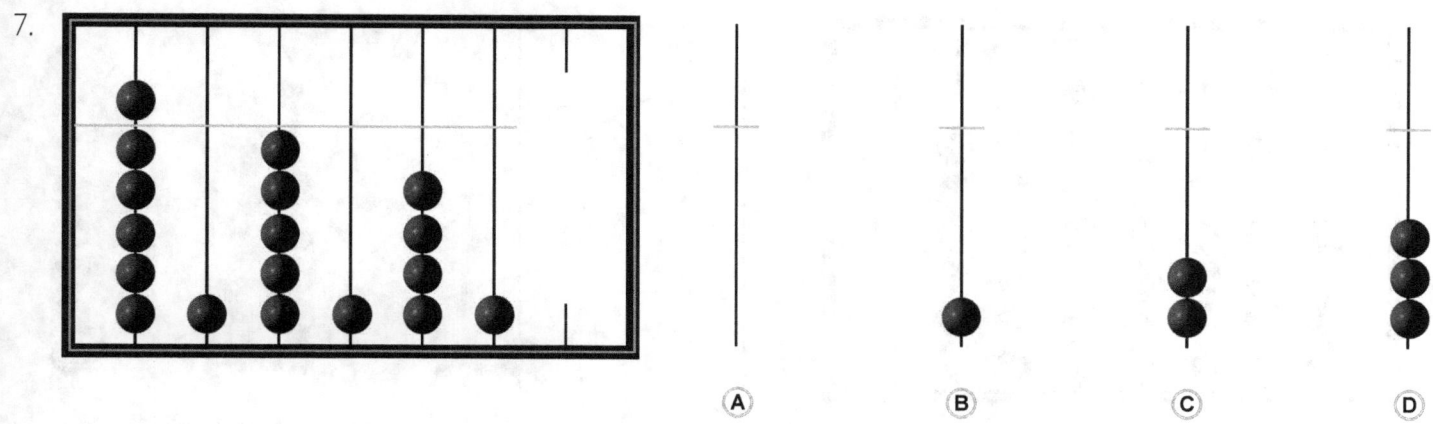

Ⓐ      Ⓑ      Ⓒ      Ⓓ

**8.**

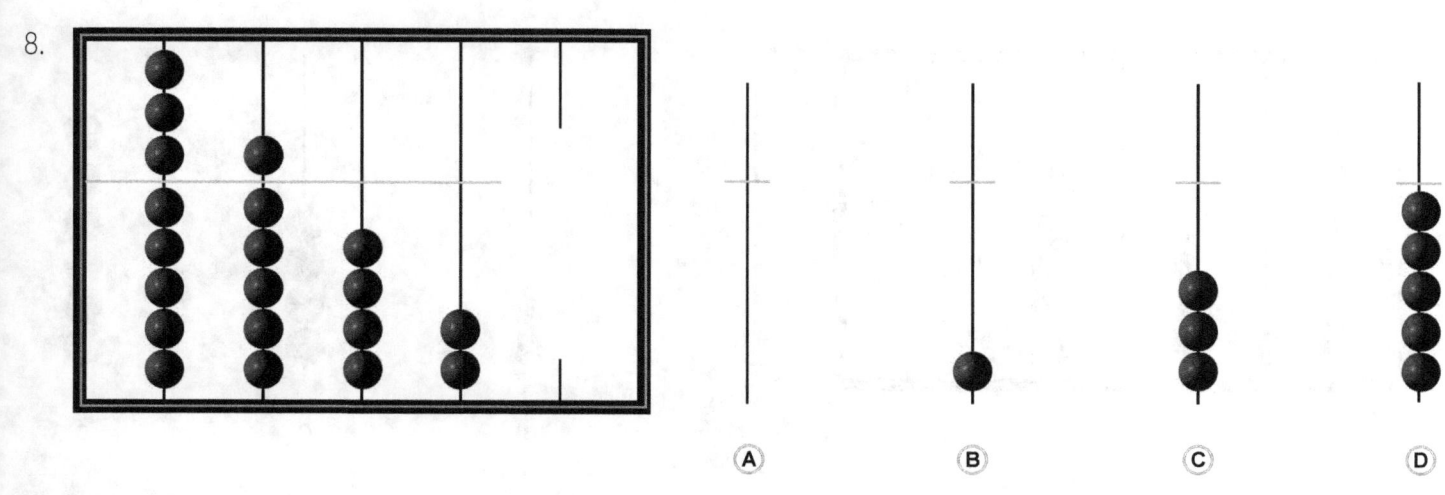

Ⓐ      Ⓑ      Ⓒ      Ⓓ

**9.**

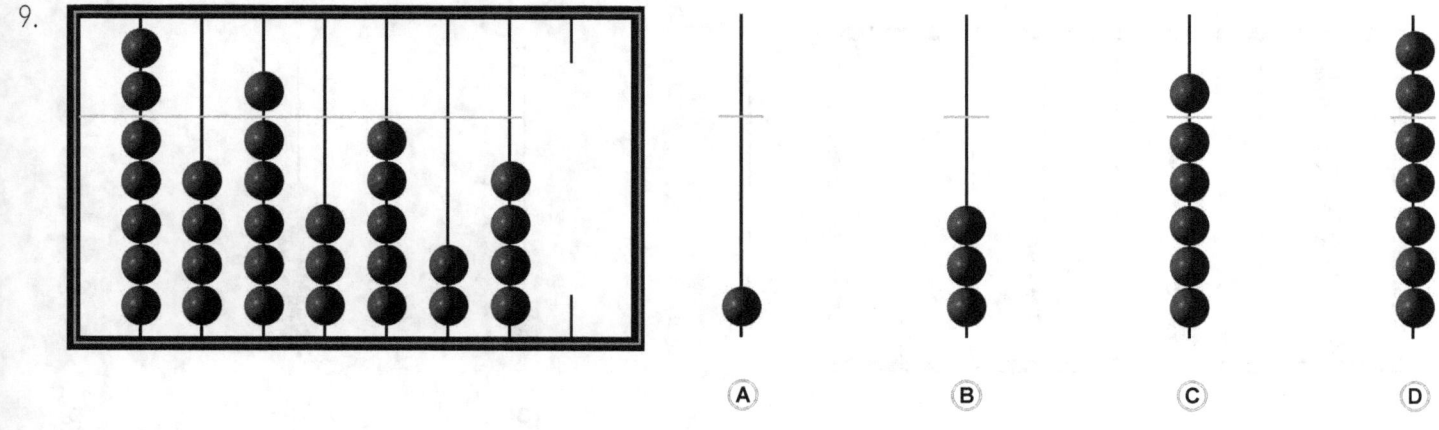

Ⓐ      Ⓑ      Ⓒ      Ⓓ

10.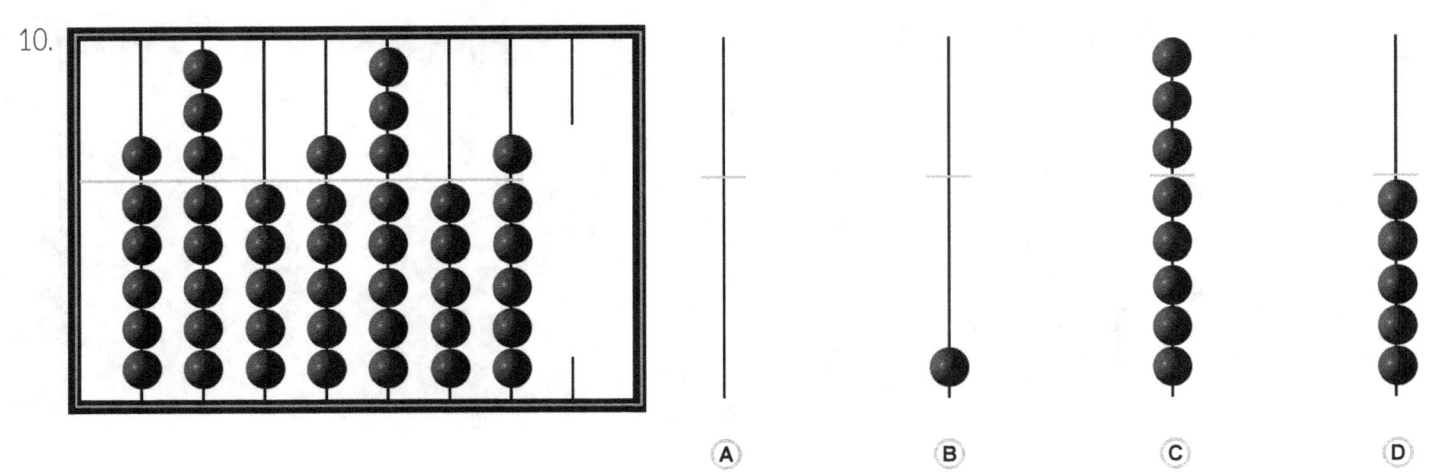

11.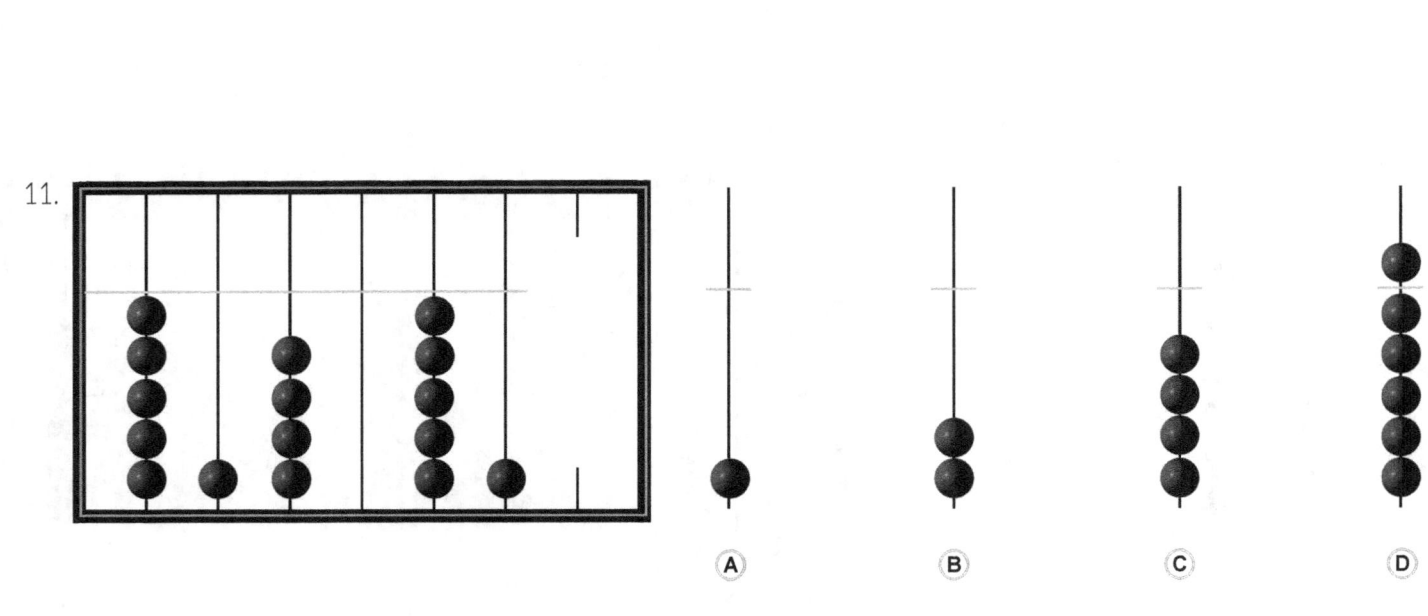

12.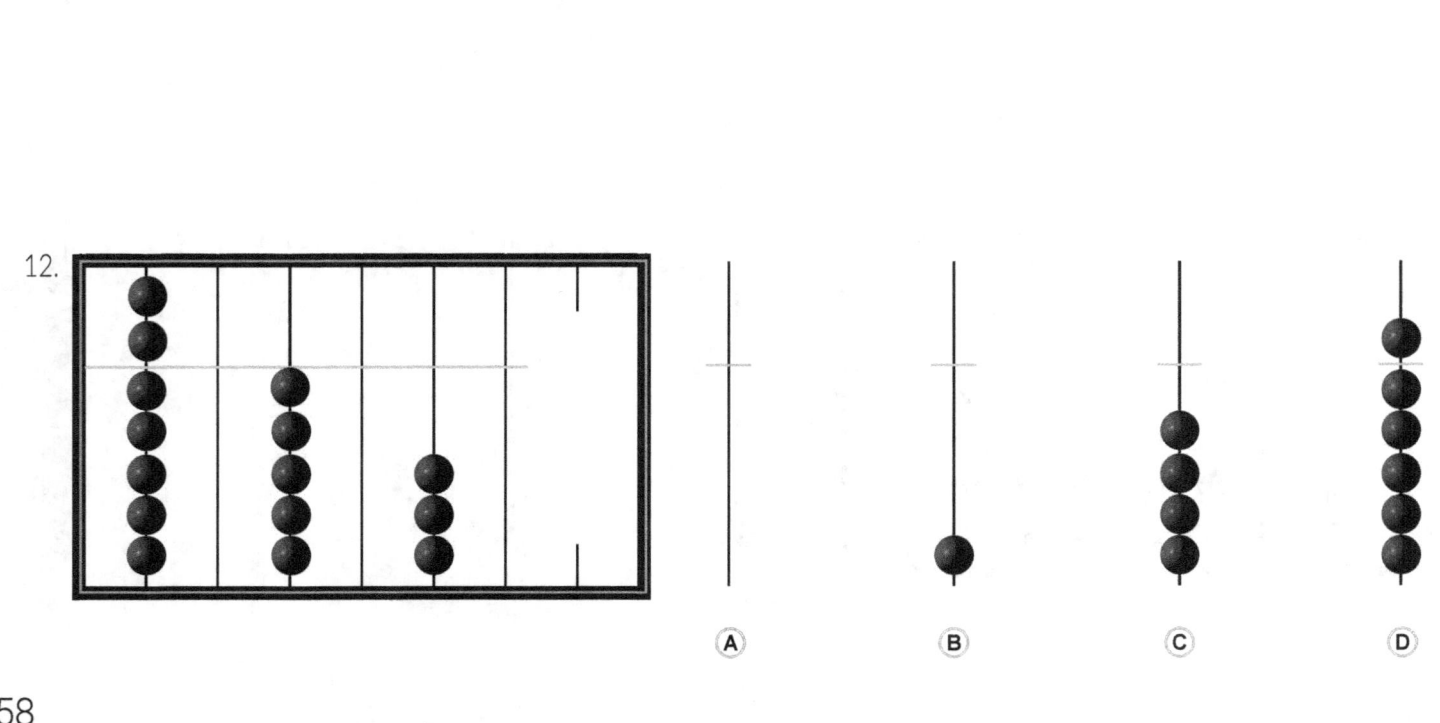

58

13.

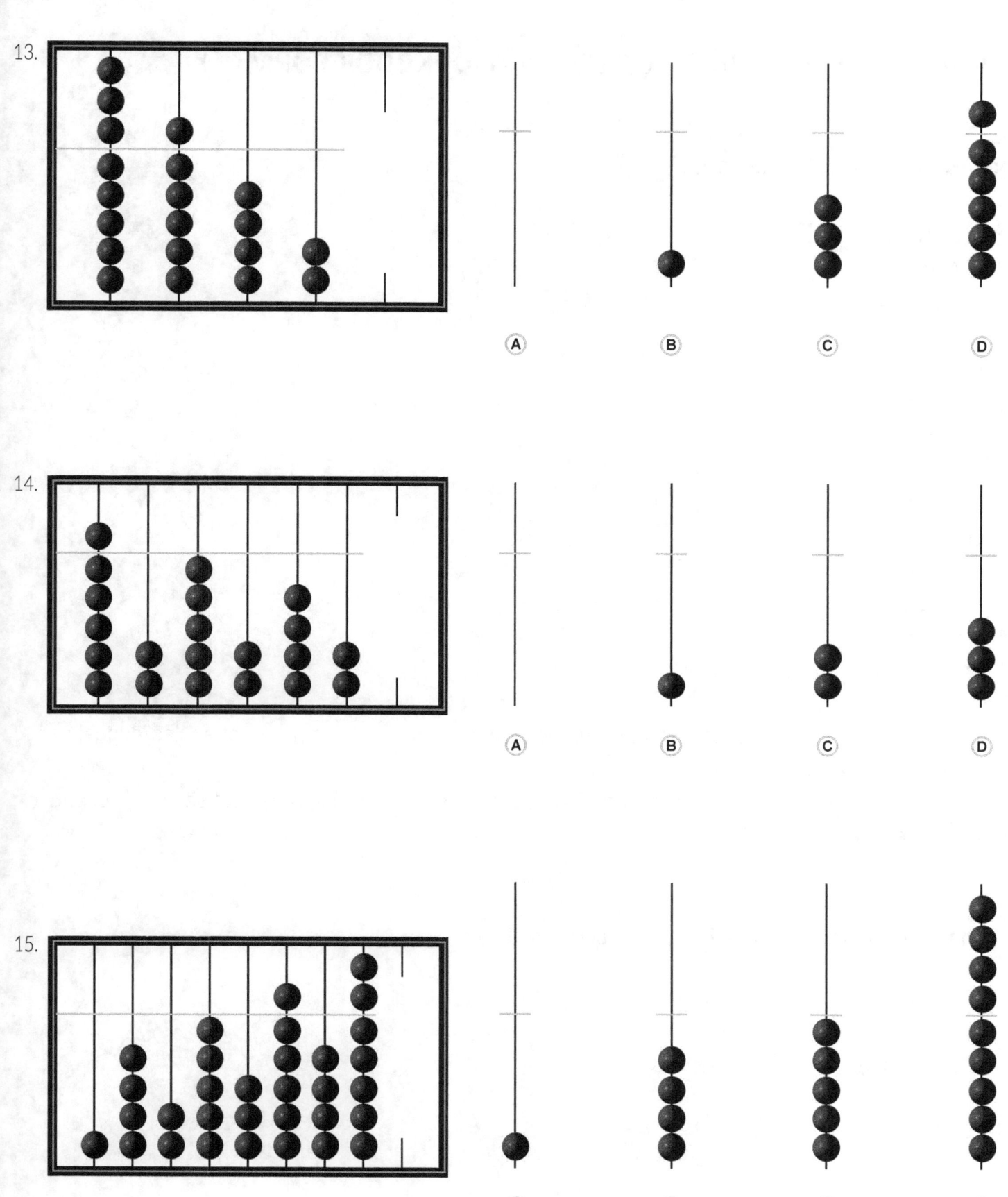

A   B   C   D

14.

A   B   C   D

15.

A   B   C   D

- The Answer Key begins on the next page. -

# ANSWER KEY FOR PRACTICE TEST 1 (WORKBOOK FORMAT)

## Number Analogies, Practice Test 1

1. B. Subtract 2.
2. A. Add 3.
3. C. Subtract 5.
4. B. Same.
5. A. Double.
6. A. Subtract 5.
7. D. Add 3.
8. A. Add 5.
9. C. Subtract 5.
10. B. Same.
11. C. Half.
12. D. Half.
13. C. Half.
14. A. Same (a shape divided in half).
15. A. Double.
16. D. There are 5 apples/cupcakes in the first box. There are the same number of apples/cupcakes in the second box, but they are split 2 and 3.
17. A. There are 4 pears/fish in the first box. There are the same number of pears/fish in the second box, but they are split 2 and 2.

## Number Puzzles (Train Questions), Practice Test 1

|  | Train 1: | Train 2: |
|---|---|---|
| 1. B. | 4 + 2 = 6 | 3 + 3 = 6 |
| 2. A. | 5 + 3 = 8 | 2 + 6 = 8 |
| 3. C. | 6 + 3 = 9 | 9 |
| 4. C. | 8 | 4 + 2 + 2 = 8 |
| 5. D. | 3 + 2 + 4 = 9 | 5 + 4 = 9 |
| 6. C. | 3 + 4 = 7 | 0 + 7 = 7 |
| 7. D. | 5 + 3 = 8 | 1 + 7 = 8 |
| 8. D | 0 + 7 = 7 | 0 + 7 = 7 |
| 9. C. | 4 | 5 − 1 = 4 |
| 10. C. | 3 | 4 + 1 − 2 = 3 |

## Number Puzzles (Train Questions), Practice Test 1, continued

| Train 1: | Train 2: |
|---|---|
| 11. A. 5 | $4 + 3 - 2 = 5$ |
| 12. A. 2 | $5 - 3 - 0 = 2$ |
| 13. B. 4 | $7 - 2 - 1 = 4$ |

## Number Patterns (Abacus Questions), Practice Test 1

1. B. There are two of each number: 6 – 6 – 7 – 7 – 4 – 4.
2. A. Every other rod has zero: 5 – 0 – 3 – 0 – 1– 0.
3. C. Each rod decreases by one: 7 – 6 – 5 – 4 – 3 – 2.
4. D. The pattern is one-one-four: 1 – 1 – 4 – 1 – 1 – 4.
5. C. The pattern is five-three-one-zero, and then reverses: 5 – 3 – 1 – 0 – 1 – 3.
6. C. The pattern of six-two-four repeats: 6 – 2 – 4 – 6 – 2 – 4.
7. C. The pattern of five-one-four repeats: 5 – 1 – 4 – 5 – 1 – 4.
8. C. The pattern of one-zero-two repeats: 1 – 0 – 2 – 1 – 0 – 2.
9. C. The number repeats three times: 1 – 1 – 1 – 3 – 3 – 3.
10. B. Each number repeats twice: 4 – 4 – 3 – 3 – 2 – 2 – 1 – 1.
11. D. Each number increases by two: 0 – 2 – 4 – 6 – 8 – 10.
12. C. Every other number increases by 1: 1, 2, 3, 4 -and- 3, 4, 5.
13. D. Every other number increases by 1: 0, 1, 2 -and- 4, 5, 6.
14. A. The pattern of four-three-two repeats: 4 – 3 – 2 – 4 – 3 – 2.
15. C. The pattern of zero-one-five repeats: 0 – 1 – 5 – 0 – 1 – 5.
16. C. Each number is repeated: 2 – 2 – 4 – 4 – 6 – 6.

# ANSWER KEY FOR PRACTICE TEST 2

**Number Analogies, Practice Test 2**

1. C. Subtract 2.
2. A. Add 6.
3. D. Double.
4. D. Double.
5. B. Half.
6. B. Half.
7. C. Subtract 5.
8. C. Full (or, nearly full) becomes empty.
9. D. There are 6 apples/pens in the first box. There are the same number of apples/pens in the second box, but they are split 4 and 2.
10. C. There are 3 rabbits/insects in the first box. There are the same number of rabbits/insects in the second box, but they are split 1 and 2.
11. C. Same.
12. B. Double.
13. D. One more section is filled in. (Or, one less section is white.)
14. D. The container changes from empty to almost full.
15. B. The container goes from nearly full to half full.
16. C. Half.
17. B. Double.
18. D. The shape changes from being all gray to half gray and half white.

**Number Puzzles (Train Questions), Practice Test 2**

| Train 1: | | Train 2: |
|---|---|---|
| 1. B. | $5 + 2 = 7$ | $1 + 6 = 7$ |
| 2. C. | $6 + 3 = 9$ | $4 + 5 = 9$ |
| 3. C. | $4 + 5 = 9$ | $6 + 3 = 9$ |
| 4. B. | $5 + 5 + 3 = 13$ | $6 + 7 = 13$ |
| 5. A. | $2 + 6 + 5 = 13$ | $8 + 5 = 13$ |
| 6. B. | $3 + 5 = 8$ | $2 + 4 + 2 = 8$ |
| 7. D. | $1 + 2 + 6 = 9$ | $3 + 2 + 4 = 9$ |
| 8. A. | $5 + 1 = 6$ | $0 + 6 = 6$ |

**Number Puzzles (Train Questions), Practice Test 2, continued**

Train 1:                     Train 2:

9. C.   4 + 0 + 5 = 9        5 + 3 + 1 = 9
10. A.  9                    2 + 7 = 9
11. D.  5                    6 − 1 = 5
12. D.  6                    8 − 2 = 6

**Number Patterns (Abacus Questions), Practice Test 2**

1. B. The pattern of 0, 1, 0, 1 repeats: 0 − 1 − 0 − 1 − 0 - 1.
2. C. The pattern of 1, 2, 3 repeats: 1 − 2 − 3 − 1 − 2 − 3.
3. C. Each rod repeats: 1 − 1 − 3 − 3 − 5 − 5.
4. A. Each rod decreases by 1: 5 − 4 − 3 − 2 − 1 − 0.
5. A. Every other rod is 0: 6 − 0 − 5 − 0 − 3 − 0.
6. B. Each rod is three of a kind: 4 − 4 − 4 − 3 − 3 − 3.
7. C. Each rod is three of a kind: 2 − 2 − 2 − 4 − 4 − 4.
8. C. The rods increase and then decrease in the same order: 3 − 4 − 5 − 0 − 5 − 4 − 3.
9. C. Every other rod increases by 1, and every other rod is 0: 2 − 0 − 3 − 0 − 4 − 0 − 5.
10. A. Each rod decreases by 1: 6 − 5 − 4 − 3 − 2 − 1.
11. B. The rods increase and then decrease in the same order: 0 − 1 − 3 − 5 − 3 − 1.
12. A. Every other rod decreases by 2, and every other rod is 1: 8 − 1 − 6 − 1 − 4 − 1.
13. D. Each rod is repeated: 3 − 3 − 0 − 0 − 2 − 2.
14. B. Every other rod increases by 1 (5, 6, 7), and every other rod decreases by 1 (3, 2, 1).
15. D. The pattern repeats: 3 − 5 − 4 − 3 − 5 − 4.
16. C. Every other rod increases by 1 (4, 5, 6) (0, 1, 2): 4 − 0 − 5 − 1 − 6 − 2.
Also, there is a difference of 4 between each pair of rods.

# ANSWER KEY FOR PRACTICE TEST 3

## Number Analogies, Practice Test 3

1. C. Subtract 8.
2. B. Same.
3. C. Subtract 7.
4. B. Add 2.
5. B. One more section of the shape turns gray. (Or, one less section of the shape is white.)
6. A. The shape becomes half gray and half white.
7. C. Half.
8. D. Double.
9. D. Half.
10. A. Double.
11. C. Double.
12. D. Add 4.
13. A. There are 4 monkeys/seahorses in the first box. There are the same number of monkeys/seahorses in the second box, but they are split 3 and 1.
14. D. Double

## Number Puzzles (Train Questions), Practice Test 3

Train 1:                    Train 2:

1. D.   10              $2 + 8 = 10$
2. B.   6               $4 + 2 = 6$
3. D.   2               $4 + 2 - 4 = 2$
4. D.   0               $5 - 5 + 0 = 0$ (Or $5 - 5 - 0 = 0$)
5. A.   $3 + 1 = 4$     $5 - 1 = 4$
6. B.   $4 + 2 = 6$     $8 - 2 = 6$
7. A.   $1 + 2 = 3$     $7 - 4 = 3$
8. B.   1               $6 - 3 - 2 = 1$
9. C.   0               $6 - 3 - 3 = 0$
10. A.  3               $6 - 4 + 1 = 0$
11. C.  4               $5 - 4 + 3 = 4$
12. B.  5               $6 - 3 + 2 = 5$

**Number Patterns (Abacus Questions), Practice Test 3**

1. D. Every other rod increases (0, 1, 2), and every other rod increases (6, 7, 8).
2. D. Every rod repeats: 0 – 0 – 1 – 1 – 2 – 2 – 3 – 3.
3. A. Every other rod decreases (7, 6, 5), and every other rod increases (0, 1, 2).
4. A. Every other rod increases (5, 6, 7), and every other equals 0.
5. B. Every other rod decreases (6, 5, 4, 3), and every other rod increases (1, 2, 3).
6. B. Every other rod increases (0, 1, 2, 3), and every other rod increases (2, 3, 4).
7. D. Every other rod decreases (6, 5, 4, 3), and every other equals 1.
8. A. Every rod decreases by 2.
9. A. Every other rod decreases (7, 6, 5, 4), and every other rod decreases (4, 3, 2, 1).
10. C. The pattern repeats: 6, 8, 5.
11. C. The pattern repeats: 5, 1, 4, 0.
12. B. Every other rod decreases by 2 (7, 5, 3, 1), and every other equals 0.
13. A. The rods decrease by 2 (8, 6, 4, 2, 0).
14. D. Every other rod decreases by 1 (6, 5, 4, 3), and every other equals 2.
15. C. Every other rod increases (1, 2, 3, 4, 5), and every other rod increases (4, 5, 6, 7).

**Ready for test day?**

• Help your child **ace the test**!

• Check out **Savant Test Prep**™ books on Amazon®.